T0109481

MAGICKAL UNICORNS

FLAVIA KATE PETERS

ROCKPOOL
PUBLISHING

A Rockpool book
PO Box 252
Summer Hill
NSW 2130
Australia
www.rockpoolpublishing.com.au
www.facebook.com/RockpoolPublishing
Follow us! rockpoolpublishing
Tag your images with #rockpoolpublishing

ISBN 978-1-925682-44-1

First published in 2019

Cover and internal design by Jessica Le, Rockpool Publishing
Cover image montage by Richard Crookes
(Artwork *A Virgin with a Unicorn*, Domenichino, 1602)
Typesetting by Envisage Information Technology, Chennai, India
Editing by Lisa Macken

A catalogue record for this book is available from the National Library of Australia

Printed and bound in China
10 9 8 7 6 5 4 3 2 1

CONTENTS

Introduction vii

1. Unicorn awakening magick 1

2. Unicorn connection magick 33

3. Unicorn dream magick 61

4. Unicorn healing magick 93

5. Unicorn service magick 121

6. Spreading the magick 139

Image credits 147

About the author 149

'Well, now that we have seen each other,' said the unicorn, 'if you'll believe in me, I'll believe in you.'

– *Through the Looking Glass*, Lewis Carroll

INTRODUCTION

Awaken, dear one, from your slumber, as the unicorns call you to arise. For they have heard your wishes to spiritually evolve and to live as your authentic self. A natural occurrence stirs within, as you open yourself up to great possibilities. What you are experiencing is a great shift in your personal energy. As you begin to awaken to the higher vibrational frequency of the unicorn realm, you no longer resonate with what once interested you. This is a time of remembering, as the unicorns prepare you to take the ancient path of magick and lore.

As the unicorns present themselves, you will find you become more in tune with the song of your soul. You will begin to notice synchronicities, new doorways will open up and what no longer serves you will fall away naturally. As you connect with the unicorns, your vibrational frequency will rise to match that which you now seek. And that's when magick takes place.

This is an auspicious time, as the unicorns reveal your destiny. You have an important life purpose and are here to shine brightly. You have always felt different, and the unicorns will help you to embrace your magickal gifts and live life to the fullest. The light of your inner knowing beckons you to invite the unicorns in, as you embrace a positive attitude.

A new and magickal page has turned, as you are invited to awaken to the healing power of unicorn magick

CHAPTER 1

UNICORN AWAKENING MAGICK

Your soul doth stir from deepest sleep
Old life fades, it's not to keep
Dreams are healed, that once were taken
A promise sealed, time to awaken
New life waits upon the dawn
Rise up to greet your unicorn.

Most of us have been brought up on the mythical notion of unicorns, of magickal horses with luminous spiralling horns that captured our imagination when we were young. Maybe you could see them through the eyes of your innocence as a child, or had a unicorn as an imaginary horse that you rode wherever you went. For most adults this is where unicorns seemed to fit in, in their imagination. There, in the inner sanctum of fantasy, they had their place along with other magickal imaginary beings, such as Father Christmas and the tooth fairy.

But what if they were really real? What if everything you imagined was true? What if these pure horned horses actually exist?

Unicorns have fascinated mankind down the centuries, through stories of mythology and reported sightings. They are fantastical beasts steeped in myth and mystery, and the tales of their chivalry and super-charged magick dominated the Middle Ages.

The truth of their existence has long been disputed, but many now believe they did indeed once walk the earth. The grace and dignity of the unicorn has been honoured by nobility, royalty and the Kingdom of Scotland, until joining with England's lion to represent the United Kingdom as a national emblem. Cave paintings all over the world depict horse-like creatures with a horn protruding from the front of their forehead, which indicates the veracity of their existence.

History of the unicorn

The unicorn has always been an especially mysterious beast, and can be traced back to Mesopotamian artwork as well as Ancient Greek writings of natural history. In Roman art, the goddess Diana was often depicted as riding a chariot that was being pulled by unicorns, and they are mentioned in Old Testament pages in the Bible. The unicorn is also included in other traditions, both Eastern and Western, and actual recorded sightings were made by Alexander the Great, Julius Caesar and Genghis Khan, among others.

In ancient times when the energies were much higher here on earth, particularly during the golden age of Atlantis, unicorn sightings were frequent as many had incarnated into physical beings of themselves. Their role was to bring in and hold the energies of myth and magick, as well as the great divine qualities they radiate, so that humankind could be influenced by them, albeit unconsciously. Unicorns can be solitary creatures, and they generally kept a distant from humans unless contact was necessary for healing purposes, otherwise they sent healing energies from afar.

As time went on the energies on earth became heavier, due to humankind's loss of belief in and connection with the magickal realms. Many unicorns began to withdraw from their physical incarnation as they could not cope with such low vibrations. As they are unable to remain on the planet they chose to spread their healing magick from the fourth dimension, in which they reside.

The last official reported unicorn sightings were in the late Middle Ages. At that time Europe was obsessed with unicorns, and secret orders gathered to uncover their mysterious doctrines; the sacred truth of the unicorns was much sought after. The spiralling horn of the unicorn was the main cause of fascination, and sadly unicorns were hunted for its magickal properties. It was firmly believed that a unicorn could bring something back to life with just one touch of its horn and could heal diseases, dissolve bad karma and break curses. In the great royal houses of Europe, a servant would use a unicorn horn to touch all the food and drink on a banqueting table to test for poison. One touch of the horn would act as an immediate antidote.

Powdered horn was an exquisite luxury, and huge amounts of money were spent on acquiring them for their healing and alchemical powers, particularly by kings and popes, who wanted the magick for themselves. Elizabeth I of England is said to have paid £10,000 for a unicorn horn, which was enough money at that time to buy a large castle. The tragedy doesn't stop with the hunting for horns, because nobody realised that cut horns lose all their magick. Only horns that are thrown off due to a seasonal renewal retain their magick properties.

According to folklore, a popular trick to capture a unicorn was to lull it to sleep on the lap of a virgin maiden and then trap it in a net. The series of seven tapestries known as The Hunt of the Unicorn, most likely made between 1495 and 1505, depict a group of noblemen in pursuit of a unicorn, with the final picture showing the unicorn in captivity. However, if the hunters touched the unicorn without invitation, which was highly likely, the unicorn would have lost all its magick power.

As the field of science slowly developed, the collective conscious belief in magick waned. In the minds of humankind the unicorn became a mythical creature, and eventually all unicorns manifested into etheric form so that only the pure of heart could see and connect with them.

It's time to allow the magick to shower you again, and to remember that it's not just for children. However, because children hold many of the qualities of a unicorn, such as purity and innocence, see instead through their eyes with joy, wonder and awe. Connect again with the child within, so you can awaken to the mystical world that you once believed in. Unicorns are magickal beings that are pure of heart, and cut through the illusion of disbelief with their glowing horn. As you welcome these beautiful beings of light into your life, they will help you to see the truth in all situations and ignite the flame of magick within your heart.

Divine feminine

Having been in hiding for over 500 years, unicorns are now returning to this planet to assist in ushering in the energies of the divine feminine. For over two millennia the world has been governed by patriarchal worship, along with a masculine mindset. Before then, goddess worship and a belief in magick ruled. This was a time when nature was revered and the gods and goddesses of the old ways were honoured. Since then the balance of nature has been tipped, as well as the hearts and minds of humankind. Now is the time to bring back the natural balance of all things, and to understand that honouring an equilibrium of male and female energies in all things as well as within ourselves will enable us to embrace this new great age and to open up to our full potential.

As we move into this new era of the divine feminine, you need to move forward spiritually and open your heart in order to progress. Unicorns are able to assist you with this, and once your heart is open and you are flowing in love it will make it much easier for them to work with you.

Try this opening your heart to the unicorns exercise:

Sit in a quiet place, preferably in nature, and hold a rose quartz crystal. Bring your focus to your heart centre.

Breathe deeply in and out three times. On your in breath, breathe in love. On your exhale, breathe out love.

As you continue to breathe love in and out, imagine a unicorn appearing before you. Take notice of every detail of what it looks like. Breathe love towards the unicorn. As you inhale the unicorn breathes love back to you, so inhale its love. Breathe your love back, and as it receives your love it breathes love back to you.

Continue this heart breath back and forth until you feel your heart chakra open up to the unicorn in front of you and to the unicorn realm.

When you have finished thank the unicorn, knowing that your heartfelt presence as a gift of love have been readily accepted.

Unicorns do exist but they live in a different dimension to us, one with a much higher frequency. They can automatically access the earth plane so you can receive their healing energies and can connect with them through your imagination and your heart chakra, both of which serve as a portal to gain access to higher dimensions.

Unicorns are beautiful ethereal horses that glow brightly and look for those who naturally radiate light. They are drawn to anyone who has a positive outlook on life and who shines. The whole essence of their being is to radiate love, so they seek out those who are pure of heart. Through the universal law of attraction, in which like attracts like, unicorns will naturally flock around those who aspire to help others and to make the world a better place.

Unicorns are gentle and pure and can only work with those who have the same qualities as they have, such as:

- purity
- compassion
- dignity
- innocence
- clarity
- grace
- honour
- peace
- love

Having any or all of these qualities is like a bright beacon to unicorns, which will immediately be drawn to you. These are the pure energies of the divine feminine that the unicorns resonate with, and they are flowing in at this time. It's impossible for unicorns to commune with anyone of lower energies, for they are unable to literally sink lower than their natural frequency. This is why they seek those who have a higher energy level through positivity and an open heart.

If you have any of the above qualities unicorns will seek you out to help you hold your highest vision and goals and give you courage and faith to be the best you can be, especially in the face of challenges. They will give you the strength to have the dignity to fight for your beliefs and will reconnect you with the higher qualities of the unicorns, to enable you to become the best version of yourself that you can possibly be. Unicorns are calling everybody to rise up and harness these loving traits so that we can all unite. They are working hard in the background to remind humankind of their existence and wish to be invited back into our hearts, for that is where the magick resides.

Always be yourself – unless you can be a unicorn!

Have you noticed that unicorns seem to be everywhere, and not just ethereally? They seem to be finding their way into all walks of life. From taking over the fashion world to food, hair and make-up, the magickal horn of the unicorn seems to have touched a majority of the retail world in one way or another. This is unicorns' way of getting into the hearts and minds of the people, for unicorns wish wholeheartedly, as part of their important mission at this critical time, to be acknowledged and accepted. Each time somebody thinks 'unicorn' they light up, which will assist them by giving them a higher energy to draw from. Think how often they are helped in this way every time you go shopping: all those sparkling, glittering and colourful unicorn bags, shirts and headbands are contributing to the magick! The world is falling in love with unicorns, and it's easy to see why:

- Unicorns don't judge.
- They're full of unconditional love and just want you to be happy.
- Despite being rarely seen for centuries, they still keep their poise and remain majestic.
- They once walked this land, but now come to people in their dreams and assist from a higher dimension.
- They are presumed to poop rainbow sherbet.
- They use their horn mostly to heal others.
- They smell like sunshine and friendship and they open up your imagination.
- They can manipulate the power of rainbows and will often exert this power to rescue those in need.
- All they desire is for everyone to find true happiness and true love.
- They help you understand the power of dreaming and believing in yourself.

Can you imagine what a magickal world it would be if everyone believed in unicorns? If everyone's heart was open to the magick and mystery of the unicorn realm, the world would be a very different place.

Here are some ways to keep unicorn vibes here, high and out there:

- *Authenticity*: unicorns don't like fakery, so always be true to who you are and to your beliefs.
- *Creativity*: unicorns love to express themselves, so go draw, paint or do whatever it takes to express the artist within.
- *Playfulness*: fun and play is the unicorns' way to raise vibration and have a jolly good laugh.
- *Compliments*: be nice to others and pay compliments, where they are deserved, to lift the mood.
- *Positivity*: having an optimistic attitude will attract all the good things in life to you.
- *Meditation*: will assist in achieving mental clarity and connection with the unicorn realm.
- *Wishes*: making wishes keeps your energy elated while waiting for the desired outcome.
- *Dressing up*: dress like a unicorn to really attract unicorn energy and cheer up those around you as you spread some unicorn magick. Dressing as a unicorn will certainly raise the vibrations wherever you go, as well as a few eyebrows! You'll need:

- Onesie: to get the full unicorn look in one. Made of soft fabrics complete with hood, horn and hooves, this really is the easiest and most comfortable way to rock your unicorn look. From sparkling white to rainbow, purples and baby pink, there are colours to suit every unicorn out there.
- Glitter: give yourself a mythical glow with glitter make-up and soft baby hues for your brows, eyes, cheeks and lips. There are lots of stunning unicorn looks out there as well as online tutorials. There's no excuse not to get glitter bombed in the name of unicorns.
- Tail: there are plenty of colourful synthetic tails out there to wear and swish.
- Horn: from floral horned hairbands to stunningly gorgeous handcrafted uni-horns that literally stick on your forehead, it's never been easier to look horny.

And if you're lucky enough to own your own horse, why not transform it into its uni-self with accessories especially for horses, such as horse-friendly glitter paint for hooves and clip-on horns.

Unicorns are beautiful ethereal beings of light that look like horses apart from one very obvious and famous feature: the horn. Unicorns are well known for their spiralling horn of light, which shines from their brow chakra; it has fascinated mankind for centuries. The horn holds pure divine energy, and can be used very much like a magickal wand. Whenever a unicorn nods its head the spiralled horn creates a vortex of energy that can be directed towards or placed upon anything that requires healing or blessings.

A unicorn's horn has the ability to unlock any blockages, and whenever a unicorn directs it healing takes place for whatever's required, whether it's on a physical, emotional or soul level. A unicorn's horn has the ability to dissolve and heal the deepest soul wounds, and can help clear karma from many lifetimes. Never underestimate the gentle power of unicorns, for these really are kick-arse horses of supernatural status with a mission to raise the roof on this planet and make sure we all ascend!

Unicorns naturally gravitate towards those who have a higher perspective on life, and just love to hang around those who are upbeat and positive. Unlike your guardian angels, who are assigned to accompany you wherever you go, unicorns can only reside within energy that is light and bright. So if you were to go into a dark and dingy bar, for instance, where the energy is lower and more basic, the unicorns would not be able join you for a quick one.

It is impossible for unicorns to lower their energy in order to fit in with what you are doing. They can only cope with energy that is as near to theirs as it possibly can be, which is why they seek those who have similar qualities to their own. Unicorns remind you that whenever your vibrations are high you cannot help but attract positivity into your life, and they will assist and work with anyone who aims at being the best they can possibly be.

Unicorns could never work with anyone who acts as a victim. They cannot abide anyone feeling sorry for themselves for they know how a pity party can have a downward spiral effect, ending in despair. Even though unicorns radiate compassion, they look for those who have the determination to dig themselves out of their self-made hole, rather than feeling sorry for those who would prefer to lick their own wounds in self-pity.

Sometimes it is extremely hard to not play the role of victim. When things have not gone your way, how many times have you blamed another for your misfortunes? If things go wrong do you immediately point the finger and say it is someone else's fault? It is so easy to do.

Before you can walk in the light you have to face the darkness, but it is unicorns that will spill the light on what is hidden – and they do not favour victims! Victimhood does you no favours either, for it keeps your focus on the negative, and a 'woe is me' attitude will keep you in a place of deep despair. You are what you create, and it is impossible to gain a sense of power in your life if your identity becomes that of a victim.

Unicorns urge you to be responsible to yourself and for your reactions, as they know how emotional upheaval and inner trauma can lead to self-pity. When you repeat over and over stories of your dramas to fuel attention, you are in fact denying yourself a happy and fulfilled life. Sob stories not only invite negativity, they can also be a bore for others to endure. They reaffirm all of the distress that needs to be dissolved, thus creating more of the same. It is time to change your story!

If you have a victim mentality you need to take steps to break out of it. Unicorns ask you to look for a deeper meaning and understand the lesson the situation is trying to teach you. In times of trouble, ask yourself what lessons you can learn. Work on eliminating any feelings of frustrations, and release any expectations you have on those around you.

By acknowledging and then releasing any conditioned thoughts and expectations, you will find that the victimised, paranoid feelings that inevitably always arise will soon dissolve, and ultimate freedom will beckon as you fuel your weary mind with the positive expectations and peace it craves.

Boo hoo, it's not fair!
It's their fault, they just don't care
Misery invites the victim in
A lack of self-belief won't win
Comply! Ditch this phenomenon
Whining victim, now begone!
It's not welcome, show it the door
The battle's over now, victor!

Unicorns encourage us to be positive and look for the best in everything.

Unicorn healing empowerment

Unicorns' energy is both transformational and healing, and works with you on a deep soul level. They remind you that in order to reclaim your power you must remember who you really are.

Unless you have healed from broken patterns of the past, you will repeat them until you are freed. Although you are experiencing a new lifetime in the here and now your life actually mirrors your past lives, and that includes the people you meet and love. Have you ever met somebody and felt as though you'd known them forever? Did you feel an overwhelming familiarity and intense rush of energy when you met your previous lover or current partner? If you answered yes, it's because you know them on a soul level.

Before each new lifetime you agree on whom to meet up with during that lifetime, what your role will be and what you need to do in order to heal and transcend. You have already previously met in other lifetimes all the people you know in this one. Incredible, isn't it? And they will act out their previous roles relative to this day and age, until you get whatever lesson you need to learn.

Unicorns help you see through the illusion of how you perceive your reality, and to understand the reason why you chose to be born into a particular family, why you are with a certain partner, your career and so on. That's right: you chose the life you are meant to live in order for your soul's growth and expansion. Unicorns see the blueprint of your story and know exactly who you are and why you are here, and as you work with them they will nudge you with hints and reminders in order for you to reclaim your power.

Are past hurts affecting the way others see you? Don't settle for second best, and never allow anyone to mistake your kindness for weakness. If you are a sensitive person then you may be rather susceptible to emotional injury. Perhaps you have always worn your heart emblazoned on your sleeve for all the world to see. This only leaves you wide open to criticism, verbal attack and judgement, and it can be a shock when you discover that not everyone is as kind as you are. Perhaps you have put your trust in those who have gone on to lie to, cheat and betray you. If you get easily hurt and find it hard to brush off any negativity that is directed your way, look deeper into the situation. It's time to trust your inner radar and not allow your emotions to run the show.

Unicorns can shield you from the harsh energies of others, as well as negative situations. They will ensure that you are not weighed down with conflicts, and will highlight issues of revenge and anger. They warn you to not let things get out of control, and encourage you to let go of old grudges and patterns that need to change. There is no way forward unless the cycle is broken. Everything that arises for you to deal with in this lifetime does so because it wasn't resolved in a previous life. However, the moment an issue is cleared up you will be released and it won't reappear in this lifetime or any other.

Everything that is thrown at you in life is thrown at you to help you grow. You cannot evolve until you acknowledge each lesson. Seeing everything from another person's perspective also works well, and unicorns can assist you with this. They love peace and harmony, and will always steer you in that direction if discord can be at all avoided.

Unicorns will hold you in their power the moment you realise the need to break free. As you release anything that does not serve your higher purpose, be open to ridding yourself of emotional attachments and undoing any vows you've made in any lifetime that have prevented you moving forward. Have you held on to something for too long, knowing it should be released but you can't quite let go? Sometimes you will hold on to hurts as a reminder to yourself to never allow the situation to happen again, or as a defence or crutch to lean on. But in your heart of hearts you know you should forgive, forget and move on, which is necessary in order to feel truly alive, to be raised up and be in your power.

The strength of unicorns is empowering and strong enough to transmute any guilt, shame, fear and blame that needs releasing. The unicorns invite you to step out from the shadows of the past and claim the life you chose in the here and now. If you feel you need to break free from any emotions that are keeping you tied to the past, here is a unicorn empowerment ceremony that will enable you to break free and become empowered and have a new sense of freedom. You will need:

- unicorn picture or figurine
- red candle
- piece of paper
- pen
- bowl

Place a picture or figurine of a unicorn in front of you. Light the candle and say:

Unicorns, I call upon you
To eliminate all in my life that's not true
Heal and diminish my guilt, fear and blame
Set them alight in the bright of the flame.

Tear the piece of paper into large pieces. Write on each piece a word that represents what you would like eliminated from your life, such as anger, jealousy or depression, or write the name of a situation or person or anything from the past that you'd like to release. Bring your focus to the candle, and watch the orange golden light flicker on top of the red wax.

Carefully hold one piece of paper at a time in the flame until it has disintegrated. At the same time, the unicorns will assist you to eliminate and transmute the negativity in your life. Put any remaining fragments of paper in the bowl. When each is done, blow out the candle carefully and say:

Protected by unicorns of love and purity
The past is released and I am set free.

It is time to rise and see the truth from all perspectives as you heal on an emotional and deep soul level.

Now that you've released that which has been holding you back and have stepped into your personal power, the unicorns will be more able to work with you. As your perception alters to a new state, your old reality will shift and feel out of alignment with how you are now experiencing the world. Allow yourself to be open to the magick of the unicorns as you start to see the world through their eyes.

Unicorn awakening

Whenever unicorns hear your soul's cry for freedom they will light you up and take you through a transformational process of awakening. But be warned, for it could seriously change your life – for the better! A unicorn awakening is rather like swallowing a pill that tears through the veil of illusion. If you are prepared to have all that you think you should have and all that you think you know stripped away to be replaced by a much older and ancient knowledge, wisdom and magick, then you are ready to embrace your soul's knowing.

Perhaps unicorns are already assisting you with the transformation your soul craves and you've already started to rise up. If so, you may be able to identify with some of these signs of a unicorn awakening:

- **Authenticity and truth**: having built up and worked towards goals for your future, it all now seems to be a bit false. You're not sure what your beliefs and values are any more, and you may have come to the conclusion that you've been influenced by the beliefs and ideals of others. Being true to yourself is most important and you cannot bear liars. You hate faking it, and refuse to wear the old masks that used to present you as someone else. You want to be completely authentic now, and can't bear those who are egotistical or show-offs.

- **Society**: you find you can no longer abide frivolous chit chat, and prefer people to get straight to the point to avoid lengthy conversations that leave you feeling restless and frustrated. Conversations that don't fulfil you will seem pointless, and you will soon notice that many people are unable to speak with truth, meaning and soul. Success, materialism and work targets mean nothing to you. You have no desire to meet social expectations and would rather not take part in the facade of daily life. As social contact decreases, you may find you lose touch with old friends. Surprisingly, they will fall away naturally as new people who resonate more with your newfound interests and passions enter your life.

- **Empathy and compassion**: as you awaken to the unicorns so will your empathy, and you now find it hard to cope with the intensity of your feelings. You find that you've developed a deep compassion for others as your attention is drawn to the perceived afflictions of the world. Be careful not to stuff down your emotions with addictive substances such as sugar, alcohol or drugs to numb the pain; instead, try to observe whether the feelings you are experiencing are yours, and if not ask the unicorns to light up those people or situations that need healing.

- **Alone time**: whereas you may once have been a party animal and the centre of attention, now you prefer to hide away. Craving solitude is a natural part of awakening as you start to experience the introverted side of your nature. Time alone is just what your soul craves as you enjoy the silence of your inner sanctum.

- **Meaning and purpose**: endless questions about your life purpose arise and you begin to read spiritual and self-help books to feed your soul. A sudden concern to fulfil your destiny takes priority as you take steps to understand the reason you are here and what you were born to do. Having worked hard for years to get qualifications and build your career, it now feels insignificant to you. You no longer feel fulfilled and desperately crave something with more meaning, something that satisfies your very soul. You wish to make a difference in the world, and your job just isn't cutting it.

- **Negativity**: although you once enjoyed a good gossip in the past, you find it almost impossible to join in such conversations. You understand the karmic law of what goes around comes around and would not wish harm on anyone, whether it's verbal or physical. Expectations of others is lost, as is your interest in conflict and drama, and you refuse to engage in anything that causes negative outcomes. You are more able to observe your own flaws and are doing your best to keep your opinions positive and upbeat.

- **Anxiety and depression**: often the shock of so many rapid changes can leave you feeling rather unstable. Periods of depression or bouts of anxiety are absolutely natural as you adjust to the new you and the completely different way you view the world.

- **Intuition**: as your energy levels rise to the higher frequency of the unicorns, you start to become aware of your inner voice and begin to trust it to guide your decisions. You become drawn towards eating a cleaner, healthier diet such as a plant-based one, and find that your intuition really starts to hum as your energetic vibration heightens.

- **Synchronicity**: serendipitous occurrences and déjà vu experiences increase as you notice the signs, symbols and omens that present themselves as signposts to direct you in life. When you understand their meanings and take action accordingly, life will become receptive and its gifts will flow more easily to you.

- **Wonder**: everything seems magickal and fascinating. Suddenly miracles are everywhere, and you feel joy from the simplest of things as you embrace the wonder of life.

- **Love**: you begin to love yourself and allow your barriers to break down, enabling your heart to love others without expectations and conditions. You understand that we are all interconnected and are all fragments of that one love, and yearn to help make the world a better place. You wish for everyone to understand and feel the wholeness.

If you concur with just one of the many signs of awakening then know that the unicorns have singled you out, because they have heard the call of your soul to be the best that you can be; they recognise your positive attitude; and they recognise their own qualities of grace, dignity, compassion and love within you.

It is time to acknowledge the spiritual truth of your awakening as the unicorns prepare you to connect and work with the power of their healing and magick. Try this unicorn awakening meditation:

Take to your bed at the magickal time of dusk. Close your eyes to invite your imagination in, and take three deep breaths in and out. Visualise a sparkling white or rainbow light around you for protection as you call across the multifaceted dimensions of the universe, and say:

Unicorns rise! I call unto you.
Awaken and assist me in all that I do.
I invoke your magick to connect us as one.
By the power of purity, there, it is done.

See in your mind's eye a group of majestic, glowing white unicorns stepping towards you. You dare not touch them, for you know all too well that one can only do so upon invitation. But one unicorn comes to you and lowers its head until the magickal horn from its snowy white forehead touches your heart.

Immediately you gasp as an intensity of love such as you have never experienced before flood through, and you feel your heart chakra begin to swirl. You breathe deeply in and out as your heart churns, and the love you feel is in epic proportions. There is no ending and no beginning, just a huge love of which your heart is an infinite vessel.

The unicorn lifts its head and looks you directly in the eyes. As you gaze into these pools of wisdom an understanding washes over you. The love you are now connecting with has the power to overcome anything that stands in your way to becoming all that you can possibly be. You have the ability to share this love, and with it will come the magick you have been wishing for; it's just you have been looking in the wrong places.

Feel your power rising up and allow the awakening of it. Vital energy surges through you, and you feel every part of you come alive as each cell and every particle resonates with the healing vibration of magick. Breathe it in deeply as you become attuned with the natural gifts of your mystical self. This is a time to receive. Allow yourself to be willing to accept these gifts that are your birthright, and fully embrace your natural and very powerful ancient wisdom, knowing and healing. Be still as the unicorns integrate with you on a full cosmic level.

You have worked with these magnificent creatures in many lifetimes before, and know each other on a deep soul level. Your relationship with the unicorns is still as strong; it is only in recent incarnations that you have forgotten. Allow the unicorns to remind you as you rest in their healing magick and remembrance. As you become sleepy, the unicorns take you deep and prepare you to meet them in your dreams, where they continue to work on you with their healing magick through the night.

Sleep and rest well, dear one, knowing that in the morning you will awaken fully restored and all set to work with the magick of unicorns on all levels.

Sweet dreams ...

CHAPTER 2

UNICORN CONNECTION MAGICK

Ancient woodland, mystic mists
Pure white horses, secret trysts
Share in magick, connect, confide
Take a magick journey ride
Soul to soul, heart to heart
A guide for life, ne'er to depart.

Excited? You should be! For you have heard the unique call of the unicorn resound across the universe through the power of your heart. You have been chosen by these magnificent creatures to help with their special planetary mission, and they invite you now to open up to receive as you learn how to connect, commune and work with them on a healing and magickal level.

Unicorns are keepers of myths and ancient magick that live in a different dimension to us, one that is a magickal and high energetic frequency that you can access easily through your imagination, wishes, invocation, meditation and spellwork. They love and revere all living things here on our beloved planet, Earth. Their vibration is at a much higher rate than ours, making it more difficult for us to see them with our physical eyes. However, that doesn't mean connection with them is not accessible. On the contrary: unicorns make themselves known to high vibrational people who have a passion for helping others, nature and our planet.

Unicorns feel your greatest hopes and assist in enhancing your natural magickal abilities to bring about healing and balance, if you will but ask. They know that when you are at peace and in harmony, so too is the natural world. They wish for you to be your optimum best, to be the best you can be, and breathe aspiration through their nostrils in the hope you might be inspired to become a co-healer of the universe. They have the power to bring healing and magick into the lives of those who feel the call of the unicorns in their soul.

Unicorns have watched you from afar and have waited a long time for you to connect with them, and you can do this much more easily than you probably thought. In fact, just thinking about a unicorn will draw one to you. The more you think of unicorns the more you will attract them to you, and this is a really effective way of calling them in. In fact, the more you include unicorns in your everyday life the more they shall surround you. All you need do is:

- think about unicorns
- talk about unicorns
- read about unicorns
- place unicorn statues, toys and pictures around your house
- have a desire to serve
- take steps to be the best version of yourself
- engage in unicorn qualities, such as love, compassion, purity and beauty

Unicorns always come from a higher perspective and will flock to you the moment your energies rise. It's much easier for them to connect with you, as they can't lower their energies to match yours. They come from a place of love and peace, so it's always good to stay positive and loving.

Unicorns will always come when you call them, but you may wish to do so in a more sacred way, in unicorn ceremony, to truly fuse your magickal connection. Try this unicorn connection exercise:

Light a white candle. Imagine a circle of white protective light around you. Say:

Unicorns, unicorns! I call unto you
I wish for your peace in all that I do

May beauty surround me, below and above
Connect my heart to your healing love
Magickal beings of purity
I welcome your healing to come unto me
Your gifts are in place to open my heart
Infinite healing is mine to impart
Energies rise so we can unite
Protect me from harm with your strength and might
I invoke your magick to connect us as one
In peace and love, we are blessed. It is done.

Blow out the candle and allow the smoke from the extinguished flame to wrap around you. Breathe deeply in and out as you harness the unicorn empowering energy that spreads through you, resonating with and vibrating every cell of your body with the magick, purity, beauty, peace and healing of the unicorns.

Now that you have connected with the healing magickal energies of unicorns you will become more aware of their pure presence. Stay in tune with them by keeping your vibrations high and invite them in as you go about your day, using any one of the simple techniques listed above. Unicorns remind us to follow the truth of who we are, to be our authentic selves and to keep our hearts open to divine love.

Unicorns are poised to assist you at any moment. All you have to do is ask them for help, and they will gallop immediately to your rescue. Because of the universal law of free will, unicorns are unable to intervene directly in your life without your permission. They can, however, trot around you to try to grab your attention if they want to nudge you in a certain direction.

Remember that you have to ask before they can take direct action. Take your time to connect and listen rather than doubt or wonder, and find inner quiet. Here you will experience thoughts, pictures or gut feelings from your unicorn to honour and act upon. They will wait patiently for you to do so, giving the odd nudge or nuzzle from time to time.

Asking unicorns for help

There is no such thing as time or space limitations to unicorns, which means they can assist many people at the same time no matter where in the world they are. Unicorns see through the illusions of your dimension and help you to open your eyes to your self-made limitations. They have the ability to act very much like guardian angels in the fact that they can offer help and assistance to those who ask.

You can ask the unicorns for anything at all. They will help you to manifest your desires, make your wishes come true and assist with anything from relationships to careers. Of course, unicorns see everything from a higher perspective and will only help out if your requests are for your highest good and purpose. Their priority is to make sure you are at peace. While you are in places of doubt and fear you aren't focused on your life's purpose or keeping your frequency high. Unicorns wish for you to experience pure peace, for when you are in a place of peace your love radiates out into the world and offers healing in the highest form.

Whenever you could do with some help or assistance just ask the unicorns. Go on; don't be shy! Unicorns love to help out, and are waiting for you to ask. They don't mind how you ask them, just so long as you do. The words don't have to be fancy; they just need permission from you in order for them to act. If you have a task for the unicorns, here are a few examples of how you can make your request:

- *Say it*: ask the unicorns out aloud.
- *Think it*: ask silently in your mind; the unicorns will hear you.
- *Visualise it*: whatever you imagine is seen by unicorns, so see your request in your mind in as much detail as you can.
- *Affirm it*: affirmations are positive statements that declare something is so and therefore it becomes so.
- *Write it*: when you put actions into a request, it becomes all the more powerful.

Whichever way you choose to ask, the unicorns will get to work straight away. Your happiness is their priority, so don't ever waste time worrying that your request will go unanswered. Doubts that the unicorns will grant your wish will block your reward, as will second guessing how it will manifest and when. Once you've made your request to the unicorns, relax and let them get on with the task as you go about your day, knowing that all is in hand.

You may not realise the unicorns are working hard in the background, until you notice a sign. Sometimes unicorns will leave physical signs to acknowledge a request to let you know they have received or are working on it. At other times they may send you signs to remind you of their presence, such as:

- white feathers: just like angels, unicorns will leave white feathers as a calling card
- white flowers: unicorns love white flowers, particularly lilies
- roses: a symbol of the divine feminine and love
- figurines/toys: you may be gifted a unicorn soft toy or a statue or drawn to purchase one
- clothes: a person may walk past you wearing a unicorn t-shirt or something similar

- billboard: you may see a unicorn emblazoned on a billboard, truck or pub sign
- white horses: a physical representation of unicorns

Often when unicorns wish to connect with you for whatever reason they will send you a sign to remind you that they're around. If you have been feeling their call and wish to get closer to them, they will let you know they're not far away.

A client of mine drove a couple of hundred kilometres to have a unicorn healing session with me, and on the way she saw a truck that had the word 'unicorn' emblazed on its side. She knew it was a sign from the unicorns that they were waiting for her. On her return journey she passed a field that was filled with white horses. They all galloped towards her car as she slowly drove past in awe, and she instantly knew it was a sign from the unicorns and that they were supporting her.

Unicorns love the purity of white, so if you wish to invite unicorns into your home why not place white flowers around your house? A potted arum lily or a vase of white roses are perfect choices to welcome and attract them in.

Another way to connect with unicorns is out in nature. Even though unicorns hail from a different and higher dimension to us, their presence is felt here on earth. Like the fairies, unicorns are able to reside here betwixt and between the worlds.

If you wish to find and commune with unicorns go look for them where the veil is thin, making it easier to see through the dimensions:

- **Woodland**: unicorns tend to gather in ancient woodland or in mystical forest glades, especially where there are birch trees. They are drawn to birch trees, and it's easy to see why for they symbolise new beginnings, regeneration, hope and a new dawn – exactly the same qualities the unicorns are ushering in.

  Unicorns have a high regard for our trees, the wisdom keepers that hold and support birds, animals and insects. These sustainers of life are wonderful gateways to other dimensions, for the spirits of the trees are multi-dimensional.

  Do you feel the trees talk to you on some level as you walk among them? Do you speak with them or give them a hug? As a custodian of the earth, you have a responsibility to the tree spirits. How often have you sat against a tree, closed your eyes and journeyed in meditation? To be one with a tree awakens the spirit within you as you draw from its resources to support and sustain you on your quest.

- **Water**: unicorns can be found near natural bodies of water such as ponds, lakes and waterfalls. The energies of water are receptive and perfect for healing with. Unicorns love the cleansing and restorative properties of water, and nudge you to work with it to help heal and clear your emotions so you are more ready to flow naturally with life.

- **Mist**: unicorns appear through the swirling white mists of early dawn, and have often been sighted through the mystical mists of the Highlands of Scotland and the Somerset Levels near Glastonbury in England.

Take some time out for you and go hunting for unicorns. Go into nature and really explore some of the mystical and ancient groves, water bodies and other magickal places near you. Sit with your back against a birch tree. Open your heart to the unicorns and let them know your intentions. Even if you don't manage to spot one, you can be sure that your request was heard and that unicorns will be making their presence known in your life.

It's not always convenient to go out searching for unicorns when you wish to commune with them, but fortunately you don't really have to go far at all. Because everything is interconnected you can connect with the unicorns at any time and anywhere.

Unicorn crystals

Crystals are gifts from the stars that are imbued with cosmic healing properties. They are packed tightly with elemental spirit and can be used to enhance communication with higher beings such as unicorns. Unicorns understand that all of nature is alive, that all beings have spirit. It is this life force, which runs through the mineral kingdom, that we all benefit from when needed.

Crystals have the power to entrance and enhance, to strengthen and energise. Working with the natural piezoelectric abilities of crystals helps you to heal deeply on a physical, metaphysical and emotional level. The crystalline energy amplifies your healing abilities, as well as assisting in a greater connection to the unicorn realm. You will find you'll become stronger and your connection amplified when you work with crystals.

Unicorns showed me many years ago that we can connect with them easily by simply holding one of the five premium crystals, which resonate with the unicorns' vibration. Working with the unicorn crystals creates a vortex of energy that allows you to connect to the pure consciousness of the unicorn realm. The five premium crystals are:

- *rose quartz*: opens your heart to the divine feminine and love, enabling you to connect with, send out and receive the healing love energy of the unicorns

- *clear quartz*: excellent for clearing blocks from the third eye chakra, and facilitates psychic connection with unicorns as well as a higher perception
- *jelly opal (girasol)*: connects you to the higher frequency of unicorns, raising your vibration for instant communication
- *selenite*: cleanses and heals negativity and fears, instilling peace and alignment with unicorn healing energy
- *snowy quartz*: has a soft feminine energy that facilitates mental clarity and alertness during meditation with unicorns

You may wish to work with one or all of these crystals to enhance your connection with unicorns. First you will need to choose your crystals or, rather, let them choose you. As you look at a selection in a store, scan your eyes across the collection until one shines up at you, or rub your hands until they feel warm and then use one to scan over the crystals to feel your way. A tingle in your hand or a change in temperature indicates you've found the right crystal.

Before you use your crystals it is vitally important to make sure they are cleansed, so you don't pick up on any other energies the crystals may have absorbed from someone or somewhere else. There are many ways to cleanse crystals; choose whichever feels most aligned with you:

- *earth*: bury your crystals in the earth of your backyard or in a plant pot
- *air*: sweep a lit incense, ring a bell or chime Tibetan bells over the crystals
- *fire*: pass your crystals quickly and safely through a candle flame
- *water*: cleanse your crystals in a bowl of water (apart from selenite, which will dissolve!)
- *full moon*: charge your crystals under its energy
- *sound*: chant 'om' over the crystals to raise their vibration

Any of these methods will clear and cleanse your crystals effectively, enabling them to lift to the highest vibration for optimum connection and communion with unicorns.

To program your crystal, hold it to your heart and take a few deep breaths to focus your consciousness and feel the connection. Hold the crystal to your third eye and say:

I programme this crystal to be used, by myself, for the purpose of communing with the unicorns, for the highest good of all.

Hold the intention, then bring the crystal back to your heart and do the following:

Breathe deeply in and out as you tune in to the crystal. Focus your attention on the crystal. Allow yourself to sink deeper and deeper into a meditative state. Feel your energy field expanding and filling with beautiful, crystalline energies. Allow your energy to merge with that of the crystal.

Feel its crystalline energy and its connection with the unicorns.

Remain in your blissful, meditative state until you intuitively know when the programming is complete. Gently move your fingers and toes and notice your surroundings. Take a deep breath in and slowly open your eyes.

Thank the spirit of the crystal and detach your consciousness from it before placing it somewhere safe.

Unicorn colours

We mainly think of unicorns as being as white as they are pure, and this is generally the case. Other familiar colours can be silver, gold and black; however, sometimes when a particular energy is needed a unicorn of another colour will appear to you, usually in your mind's eye or during meditation. Every colour has its own specific frequency, which can be harnessed as a healing energy on many levels:

- *white*: spirituality, purity, peace, faith, innocence, light, humility
- *silver*: grace, sophistication, elegance
- *gold*: personal power, courage, strength, enlightenment, wealth, passion, magick
- *pink*: compassion, caring, understanding, unconditional love
- *purple*: royalty, luxury, mystery, wealth, dignity, devotion, wisdom
- *turquoise*: refreshing, feminine, calming, tranquillity, intuition, emotional balance
- *blue*: freedom, imagination, expansiveness, inspiration, depth, sensitivity, trust
- *brown*: wholesomeness, reliability, security, grounding, stability, warmth, honesty
- *black*: power, mystery, strength, authority, elegance, formality, death, protection
- *rainbow*: comprised of the seven colours of the visible spectrum, high vibrational rainbow light clears chakras and balances feminine and masculine energies; send this energy out by wearing rainbow colours or visualising the world wrapped in a beautiful rainbow

Whenever you wear or see a colour you are influenced by its energy. So when dressing, why not choose your colours mindfully in accordance with your energetic requirements or that of those around you? As you bring colour into your life, the unicorns will also colour it up.

Unicorn names

How do you feel at the mere mention of the word 'unicorn'? Does your heart chakra open immediately to the love energy that vibrates through the sound of their very name? Perhaps you feel the purity of their energy filling you with deep peace, or maybe a mystical feeling sweeps over you as your body tingles with unicorn magick.

Every name carries a unique vibration that helps to connect to your soul. We all choose our own name prior to birth; it has the vibration of who you really are on all levels, including your life purpose and mission. On a higher level your name tells all of who you are in every aspect. It holds the key to your core wounds, gifts and talents and all that your soul chose for this lifetime. It is said that a leprechaun will never give his real name for that very reason!

Often a unicorn won't give its real name in case you can't quite yet resonate with its high frequency, or it may be unpronounceable for you. Unicorn names derive from an entirely different dimension and are not always easy for humans to understand, let alone pronounce. In these cases the unicorn will give a name that you can easily understand but still hold the energy the unicorn emits.

Unicorns will always give their names the moment you ask. Usually it is the first name that comes to you before your ego kicks in screaming that you've just made it up. Please always trust what you first get, as the unicorns will always give you something you understand.

When I first met my unicorn guide and asked for its name during a meditation I was given the name of Lavender. The name Lavender just popped into my head before I could even think about it so I knew immediately it was correct, especially as I knew that lavender is a scent they just adore! Lavender is white, pure, gentle and compassionate, and has all the other beautiful qualities of the unicorns on which I can draw love, comfort, healing and guidance. He has a completely different energy to Metropolis, a mighty black unicorn that assists me with courage, self-power and determination. He's always by my side when I'm working to support the unicorns' mission, and lends me his strength in the face of challenges.

Unicorn guides

When you have unicorns in your life you will find you are being nudged – often literally – in the right direction. You may find that brilliant ideas pop into your head, or that you have greater confidence and feel lighter and happier. If you love unicorns then they are loving you right back.

Each and every one of us has a guardian angel that watches over us and guides us towards our destiny. Those who love and resonate with unicorn energies and their qualities and have a vision beyond themselves have their very own unicorn guide as well. Unicorn guides work with you through your heart centre, and know you on a deep soul level. This means that every part of who you've ever been is accessible to them, and they know you inside out and back to front. You will also know your unicorn guide in this way. It's just that when you incarnate into human form you forget all your past-life and in between memories as you go through the veil of amnesia.

Your unicorn guide will assist you with any request you have as long as it's for the highest good of all. The guide will help you to heal on all levels in order for you to evolve, and assist you in being the best version of yourself. You may have more than one guide eventually, depending on what your soul has signed up for.

You can easily meet your unicorn guide during visualisation meditation, which grants access to dimensions including the unicorn realm. This is a wonderful way to get to know your unicorn, which may have a message for you, and you can also ask it its name. Your unicorn guide exists just for you, and is waiting to meet you in a forest clearing within ancient woodland. It's been quite a while since you sat with your guide, my friend, so take some time now to connect and become reacquainted.

You may wish to hold a unicorn crystal to enhance your experience through this meditation:

Close your eyes and breathe in and out comfortably. Imagine a circle of bright sparkling white light around you. See yourself in a beautiful forest, an ancient forest, forged in mystery and magick.

A path leads deeper and deeper into the forest, which you take as you breathe in the pure air and listen to the joyful song of the birds. The heightened scent of the flowers and pine needles makes you feel quite heady, and you realise that this forest is unlike any other.

As you look around you see mighty, majestic trees waving in the breeze and squint at the bright green leaves as the sunlight streams through. It is beautiful, and you notice that as the shafts of bright golden light shine through the trees they meet together as one blast of blinding light, just in front of you, and you are quite blinded.

Suddenly you hear sweet music and voices singing:

Dance in circles all around
Spinning magick to the sound

of music, laughter and good cheer
Celebrate, come join us here!

As though an enchantment has been placed upon you you follow the sound, which takes you into a thicket of trees. Notice the fairy energy, for tonight is the strongest time for the workings of magick. Allow yourself to be part of the magick and breathe it in. Feel it surge through you as you weave between the trees, until you come across a glade.

A huge ancient birch tree hides you as you carefully peer around its sturdy trunk and take a sneaky peak. As your eyes adjust, you blink at what you see: why, the glade is filled with fairies dancing in circles and having a wonderful time!

As you secretly watch them you feel your soul stir, connecting you to ancient times. Wishing to enter the magickal circle and join in the fun, you hold the intention for the highest good, and the desire that no harmful thing comes from your visit, and say:

As I enter within this magickal ring,
My heart is open and ready to sing
Songs of the wood, words of the fae,
Who guide me in and show me the way.

A fairy comes forward and takes you by the hand. She leads you into the middle of the fairy party in the glade. Unsure of what you should do, you stand there watching the festivities.

Suddenly a cheer goes up and a group of glowing unicorns trots into the glade. Fairies surround them, cheering and singing. It's a time for celebration! A couple of leprechauns take up their fiddles and start playing a jig:

Dance and sing, don't look forlorn
Let's welcome in your unicorn
It'll take you on a magick ride
For you've become its greatest pride.

A unicorn comes up to you, and stepping carefully towards it you immediately feel the pureness of its aura. The unicorn looks at you as though it is looking deep into your soul. You feel an unknown, profound calmness and inner peace that you have never felt before, and a wonderful closeness is felt between the unicorn and yourself.

Your thoughts cross in a silent understanding, and you feel unconditional love and devotion such as never before. A feeling of infinite wisdom and understanding flows through your body and you begin to see the world through the unicorn's eyes, a world that is full of love and light.

The unicorn nods as an invitation for you to stroke or pat it. As you do, connect with the unicorn and feel its energies of purity and innocence. This is your guide, who works with you at a soul level and has come to you now because of your desire to serve.

The guide nudges you to sit against the birch tree, then sits next to you on the spongy green moss. Tell the unicorn what you wish for in your life, and be sure to project your desires for the highest good of all.

This is a time of healing with your unicorn, to become reacquainted, so spend some time with it. What colour is it? How does its energy feel?

Ask any questions you may have; you may wish to ask its name. Tell of the longings of your soul and listen for a response, or you may want to sit and just enjoy its company for a while, to feel the love and other beautiful qualities of the unicorn.

The unicorn invites you to climb onto its back and takes you through the woodland. You emerge into sunlight, and see ahead a great doorway with beautifully scented roses growing all over it. The unicorn nudges the door gently; it swings open and the unicorn takes you through it.

Through the doorway, on the other side, there is a soft green glade full of wild flowers. It's so beautiful. You notice an ancient wishing well in the centre of the glade, and the unicorn walks towards it. Surrounding the wishing well is a carpet of hundreds of crystals: clear quartz, rose quartz, selenite, girasol and snowy quartz. Each contains properties that connect well with the unicorn realm.

You gently climb down from the unicorn and gaze at the beautiful crystals, and feel the intensity of their healing energy. As you scan the jewelled ground you are drawn to one of the crystals, which shines up at you. You pick it up and, holding it carefully, look at it. As you begin to attune to the properties of the crystal, say:

Crystal, help me shine my light
I yearn to see with second sight
Assist my healing, and in spell
Your magick serves me very well.

As the crystal sparkles and shimmers in the sunlight, you make a wish into it. Take your time to describe everything that you desire, then offer the crystal to the unicorn. Very carefully, the unicorn blesses your wish by touching the crystal with its horn. A blinding flash makes you step back

in surprise, and you drop the crystal into the well with your wish and your unicorn's blessing infused in it.

Lie back on the soft, lush grass and visualise your life as if the wish has already been granted. Relax and take care to see every little detail. See it; feel it! For this is how wishes magickally transpire into reality.

After a while your unicorn nudges you to climb onto its back, and returns you through the doorway of roses and back into the glade. As your unicorn nuzzles you say a heartfelt thank you and your goodbyes for now – for you can access your unicorn guide at any time whenever you think of it and feel it through your heart, through meditation and in your dreams.

Step carefully back into your own world, bringing with you a new sense of magick and wonder. Your life will never be quite the same again.

Still feeling the amazing energies of your unicorn guide flowing through you, take three deep breaths in and out and return, in your own time, back to your world.

Namaste.

CHAPTER 3

UNICORN DREAM MAGICK

Insight strong, gifts to receive
Sacred sight, in this believe
With eyes wide shut, fall into sleep
Journeys to take, wishes to keep
Dreams reveal what is to be
Trust in the answer, then wait and see.

The inner love light of unicorns is like moonlight: pure, receptive and illuminating. They vibrate with the feminine energetic magick contained within the moon itself, and share an open heart with those who truly appreciate the divine connection that love brings. They nudge you to make a wish upon a star, and cheer when your dreams come true. They inspire you to soar, and will accompany you as you fly high through the sky and bathe in the colours of the rainbow. As you allow the magick of unicorns in, they fully support all of your efforts in a gentle, consistent and peaceful way.

We are all spiritual beings in a physical body who have come to earth purely for the experience and to learn lessons. One of these lessons is to remember exactly that: that we all come from the stars and are one and the same, interconnected and created to perfection.

The veil of amnesia ensures you forget who you are as you birth into this realm here on earth. However, some people come in with a remembrance of who they were in past lives, and have a natural spiritual connection and believe in magick. Others are less evolved and accept the perceived illusionary way of the world as reality. Society has done its very best to ensure you don't see beyond the material offerings, and you are bombarded with high-tech gadgets to keep you busy and distracted from any spiritual connection or rescue. Television shows, movies, the internet and gaming invade that inner place of creativity, luring you into the illusion of a world of drama and conflict. It's escapism, although most people don't understand what they are actually escaping from.

As a spiritual being you don't actually truly belong here on earth. Your human body has been placed around your spiritual self rather like a space suit equipped with all the functions needed to cope with your earthly presence. We live in a three-dimensional existence, which vibrates at a lower frequency than the higher dimensional realm of the unicorns.

The energies can feel quite harsh on earth, not only for the higher beings of light such as unicorns but also for those people who are highly sensitive. If you have had more past lives in a higher frequency dimension than you've had on earth, chances are you find it hard to cope here.

Highly sensitive people view the world differently from others. They are creative, insightful and empathetic, and can easily be affected by other people's emotions or physical ailments. If you are highly sensitive other people's moods will affect you, and you often won't be able to distinguish between your own emotions and someone else's. Highly sensitives are naturally attuned to subtleties of all kinds, and a richness in things that others may overlook. They are able to draw inspiration from their complex inner lives and in turn try to create beauty, joy and inspiration for themselves and others.

How spiritually aware were you as a young child: did you have an affinity with the magick of nature? Maybe you had a strong belief in magickal beings such as fairies and unicorns, or perhaps you always felt different or special in some way and knew you were here to make a difference. If so, there's a good chance you could be a highly sensitive person. Check out the list of highly sensitive traits below:

- your heart overflows with a sadness and sorrow that's not yours
- you cry very easily
- you're sensitive to negative energies and people
- you find crowds and chaos overwhelming
- when someone tells you about their happiness or hardship you share their every emotion
- you know what people need and how they feel without them telling you
- you feel the emotional ripples of the collective consciousness
- you're a great listener
- you get tired and drained easily, especially around negative people
- you enjoy your own company
- you've had premonitions and precognitive dreams and have strong hunches
- you can sum people up within minutes of meeting them
- you find watching the news or reading newspapers upsetting
- you've always had a feeling you're different from everyone else

If you answer 'yes' to any or all of the above then you most certainly are highly sensitive, which can be very challenging for you. It's especially hard when others perceive you to be weak or silly for being so sensitive.

Have you ever berated yourself for feeling too emotional, perceptive or insightful? Perhaps you thought something was wrong with you, or maybe you worried that you had a mental disorder. This isn't unusual for highly sensitive people, who can't understand why others don't think and feel how they do. It's tough in this day and age, and pressure to be normal can be just as overwhelming as your sensitivities!

Highly sensitive people not only absorb the stresses and emotions of others into their bodies; they can also be sensitive to the effects of food. As a highly sensitive being, try not to numb your feelings or stuff down your emotions with alcohol or food. Many sensitives turn to addictive substances in order to make them feel better and to block out all the emotions they are dealing with. This can be very common, but unfortunately it dumbs down a sensitive's ability to tune into the higher realms.

If you overeat or binge on sugar, carbs or junk food when you're emotionally overwhelmed, understand that all foods carry frequency-based messages and have the ability to change your vibration according to the principles of spiritual nutrition. Eating low life-force foods such as heavily processed and packaged meals will impact the frequency of your entire being, bringing your vibrations down and low and making you feel even worse than ever. Clean, fresh, whole and healthy foods such as fruit, vegetables, nuts and seeds will raise your energy and lift your vibration on all levels, making connection access to the unicorn realm much easier.

If you are highly sensitive be very aware of what you are putting into your body, because the energy of every bite counts!

Once you understand why you feel the way you do you can take steps to embrace your sensitive side, for the truth is that sensitivity is a beautiful gift. It helps you to feel for others, to be both empathetic and sympathetic, and also opens your heart so that you are more readily able to receive the loving messages of the unicorns:

Allow us, dear one, to lift that heavy burden you have been carrying around. Because you are such a sensitive soul you naturally take on another's feelings. The problem here is that you tend to analyse what you presume to be people's emotional hurts and thoughts, and you end up torturing yourself with worry on their behalf. How often have you been unable to bear the thought of someone being on their own, not having enough money or enjoying the love you would see them have?

Surrender your fears to us and break down your barriers, as we heal your wounds and dissolve any pain. Focus on and breathe into your heart the pure divine light with which we radiate. Accept this healing as you hold acceptance and appreciation towards yourself, for these are the nutrients that feed your soul.

Love is your true nature and it is necessary for you to honour the compassion you feel in your heart. When you are true to yourself your light shines brightly with divine love, nourishing you from within and inspiring those around you. True love is unwavering, and you, we promise, are wholly cherished.

You are loved and valued unconditionally. Remember that love always has the answer, for it is the only answer!

Dreaming time

If unicorns wish to commune with you but have difficulty getting though, they will visit you when you are asleep. This is the perfect time for them to make contact with you, for while you are sleeping so too is your ego.

The function of your ego is primarily to guide you through this harsh world. It thinks it protects you from harm through the voice of your inner critic. You know, the one that says: 'Don't trust her, she hurt you last time', or 'You can't do that, there are better people out there who can.' It doesn't mean to sound negative; all it's trying to do is

protect you from getting hurt, and it works by comparing a situation to your previous experience.

The voice of the inner critic can also be quick to tell you that something you believe in is not true, or will negate it in some way or other. This is what you may hear when you are trying to meditate: a voice telling you you are making it all up, that you can never achieve what you are trying to. It is very off-putting when you want to hear the messages from the unicorns!

Quietening a noisy chattering mind can be a tough job, and makes it hard for the unicorns' loving messages to be heard. Take a moment to allow the unicorns to breathe a beautiful peace through your fragmented mind:

Light a yellow candle and take three deep magickal breaths in. As you gaze at the flickering flame of the candle, start to increase the power of your breath in and out and become aware of the air that surrounds you. Say:

Unicorns, unicorns, breathe through my mind
Purity, clarity, so I might find
Silence within, a still inner peace
Fears, doubts and worries, begone now, release!

Continue to breathe deeply. You feel your heart expand, filling with the loving energy of the unicorns. Breathing their energy in and out, start to feel your connection with them build up. Purposefully direct your breath out. Build your breath up and blow it out and up into the air. In your mind's eye your breath is a beautiful golden yellow, like spring daffodils.

As you continually breathe in and out deeply, watch as the golden yellow breath expands out across the scene in front of you. Purposefully breathe deeper still and send it out across the surrounding area. Watch or feel as it is joined by a host of unicorns, which escort this energy of new purity out across the countryside, towns and oceans and across the entire world. Allow the unicorns to do the rest as they cleanse, clear and heal the air of the planet.

As you watch, you hear sweet singing all around you:

Air sweeps in with all its might
Clarity gives you sacred sight
Imagination is the key
Unleash your gift, trust what you see.

The power of air sweeps through your imagination and urges you to believe that what you see is real, for imagination is the gateway to magick.

The unicorns enhance your focus and stimulate your mind as they turn their breath to you. Breathe it in deeply and purposefully up to your third eye in your forehead. As clarity sweeps through your imagination you will start to notice the subtle messages that the unicorns leave you, such as shapes in the clouds, whispers upon the winds or vivid colours.

Unicorns are bringers of new life, of possibilities, and they blow us in the direction of our dreams. Throw caution to the wind and trust your visions as they manifest into reality.

As a new magickal energy surrounds you, the unicorns encourage you to go grab your dreams and reach for the stars. They are poised to support you, as their hearts reflect your thoughts and intentions. Unicorns encourage you to delight in the wonder of who you are, and remind you that their magickal messages are everywhere and in everything if you will but see with a loving heart and sacred sight.

The unicorns love to connect with you during your dreams, as you have no physical limitations while you are asleep. In fact, your soul has a life of its own when you are all tucked up in your beds and are none the wiser. As your body plugs in to recharge, your soul is free to travel across the universe. You don't realise it, but as you sleep your soul visits your friends and family who live far away and you can meet up with other beings who live in different galaxies and dimensions.

Sometimes you will choose to learn while you are asleep and have access to spiritual night school. There you are taught by the mighty archangels and the ascended masters, who will impart to you all you need to know at that time as well as giving you healing on any level. You will return to your body and awaken with no memory of your nightly adventures. Any wisdom, knowledge or healing shared becomes apparent all in divine timing when needed.

Those whose purpose it is to wake up others to connect with their true divine spirit and are drawn to the spiritual side of life tend to do their healing work when they are asleep, without even realising or remembering when they wake up. I have had many lovely messages from people thanking me for my assistance in their dreams, which I have no recollection of. Once I was even paid for my nightly services: I couldn't understand where a PayPal payment had come from. I sent a message to the email that had come through with it and was thanked wholeheartedly. The payment, apparently, was for the healing services I'd given the previous night!

I always find going to bed quite exciting, for the entire universe is at my disposal. You never quite know where you are going or who you will meet. That is, unless you consciously decide to.

If you would like unicorns to enter your dreams, the first thing you need to do is ask them to visit. Hold a unicorn crystal in your hands and say:

Unicorns come and colour my dreams
Paint them with starlight and silver moonbeams
Fill me with magick, this I ask too
Please grant me a wish, that it may come true
Help me to heal and open my sight
I welcome you in, this very night.

You will need to prepare yourself for their visit first. Remember that unicorns cannot lower their energy to match that of another, so you will need to ensure that your light is pure enough for the unicorns to connect with you at a higher level. Make sure you clear and raise your energies before you go to bed, which can be done in a number of different ways.

Psychic cleansing shower. Water has incredible spiritual healing properties that promote clearing for your body, aura and consciousness.

As you stand in the stream of water, visualise it as a bright golden liquid healing light running over you. Visualise your energy flowing down, grounding you to the light at the earth's core.

As you visualise your aura, allow yourself to see any negative energy within it. Purposefully release any lower vibrations into the light. Rinse off any negativity, density and lower energy and let it all drain away down the plug hole.

When you are finished, visualise your aura and energy body as being clear and vibrant.

Give thanks to the water spirits for the clearing, and to the unicorns for their healing light and support.

Crystal shower. You can use a unicorn crystal while in the shower to help banish unwanted energies and charge up your vibration. Don't use selenite, though, as it dissolves in water!

As you stand in the water stream, see it as a golden liquid cleansing light pouring over you. Gently rub the crystal over your skin to clear, cleanse and recharge your body. Wave the crystal around and through your aura to pick up any dross energies.

When you have finished, flick the crystal into the liquid light as it flows down into the drain, taking with it all negativity. Give thanks to the crystal, and cleanse it in the shower water itself or in a bowl of salt water.

Waterfall of light. If you don't have a shower you can imagine the above processes instead at any time. Simply visualise the entire shower scene to clear and cleanse, and energetically it will be done!

Affirmations. Positive affirmations can help you overcome self-sabotaging and negative thoughts. When you say uplifting statements about yourself, believe in them and repeat them, positive change happens.

Positive mental repetitions can reprogram your thinking patterns, and when you believe in them you invite in the law of attraction which returns to you exactly what you give out. In other words, if you believe in what you have said and repeated it enough times for the universe to believe you, then it will come about. Three times is usually a good number to repeat a statement, but it really depends on how much you believe it too.

Here are some strong and positive affirmations for you to say that will raise your vibration to attract unicorns:

I am a being of pure love and light.
My light shines brightly.
I easily attract unicorns to me.

Say your affirmation enough times to feel your energy lift in response to your positivity and belief.

Chanting. Chanting is connected with ancient spiritual wisdom traditions of everlasting significance. The recitation of mantras can bring about transformation and provide you with the power to lift yourself to a higher level of consciousness. Sounds are a manifestation of energy vibrating at different frequencies, and are imbued with centuries of meaning.

'Om' is an ancient mantra that is considered to have high spiritual and creative power. When chanted it vibrates at the frequency of 432 Hz, which is the same vibrational frequency found throughout everything in nature. Om is both a sound and a symbol rich in meaning and depth, and can easily be recited by anyone. When pronounced correctly it is actually 'a-u-m', and it is the basic sound of the universe:

- *a* is pronounced as 'awe'
- *u* is pronounced as 'oo'
- *m* pronounced as 'mmm'

By chanting this sacred mantra you will tune in to your connection with the universe and acknowledge that we are all one. Chanting 'om', using a singing bowl or singing sacred songs will all raise your vibrations.

Sacred music. Music can raise your vibration, especially if it is recorded for meditation or for complementary therapy sessions. Close your eyes and listen to a CD of sacred music in bed; as you deeply relax, allow the music to raise your energy to a highly charged frequency.

Chakras. Visualise your chakras – your body's energy points – as being cleared, whole and spinning with high, vital life-force energy. (For more information on chakras, see Chapter 4.)

Protection

Once you have cleared and raised your energy levels you should put protection in place. Spiritual attacks can occur when you are sleeping because you are at your most vulnerable, so it's always best to use some form of protection to ensure your spirit has a safe journey through the night.

Divine love shield. *White light* is the light of the holy shield, one of the most powerful forces in the universe, which you can use as a protection tool. It can be invoked simply by envisioning a bright white light placed around you.

Purple light is the highest angelic vibration you can invoke for spiritual protection, nurturing and support. Use it on its own, or layer it on top of white light.

Pink light is pure heart-centred energy that expands love out to reach others and allows divine love in while blocking psychic attack. Wrap it around a white layer for ultimate protection and love energy.

Divine love. Simply focus on your heart chakra and intend for it to feel the emotion of love. As you breathe deeply and with intention, watch as your heart expands and sends out a big bubble of divine love. Watch in your mind's eye as the bubble expands until it is bigger than you are. Step into the bubble of love, which will provide you with all the protection you need: for, as the unicorns know, love conquers all!

The archangel Michael and angels. The archangel Michael is known as the leader of the archangels and can be called upon to give strength, courage and protection. He's usually seen carrying a sword of light, which he uses to cut through fear and negativity. His role is to defend and rid the earth of lower energies and he offers his protection to us as well, especially to those who work in the light for the higher good. Call in the archangel Michael to protect you or ask him to wrap you in his purple cloak of protection. Ask the angels also, as they will be happy to surround you and protect you through the night.

Unicorns. Of course, you can ask the unicorns to watch over you as you sleep. If you wish them to accompany you in your soul travel, just ask and they will be more than happy to oblige.

As you go to bed you might like to think about where you would like to visit during the night, or you could simply ask them to take you to a place they know you'd love or would benefit from. You could ask to be taken to the unicorn kingdom, or to simply spend time with your unicorn guide and get to know it better. Just put in your request by simply stating your intentions, always adding 'for the highest good of all', and know that the unicorns will connect with you once you've drifted off.

If you prefer to invoke the unicorns in a more powerful way you can use this safe, effective spell, which will colour your dreams and enhance your visions:

- Place a clear quartz under your pillow as you prepare for sleep and say:

Moon is up, magick abounds
Raise the vibes with sacred sounds
Unicorns help me to align
With the stars that brightly shine
Clear quartz placed for clarity
Dreams reveal what is to be.

- As the unicorns open the door to the realms of dreams to you say:

Protection in place, no need for fright
The unicorns keep me safe tonight
I enter my dreams with harm to none
With divine love; there, it is done.

Dream incubation

The answers you seek will more often than not come to you in your dreams and will be presented to you through the images and stories of your dreams. Dream incubation is simply focusing on what you wish to know before you go to sleep in order to get answers to your questions and to spiritually evolve.

Before going to sleep, plant a seed such as a thought or intention in your mind in order to dream a specific topic. Pre-sleep topics can be anything from asking to see finished artwork in dreams to developing plots for a novel, to solving all types of problems. In the morning you will have the answers. It is a wonderful way to tap into the consciousness of all!

Specific dreams

When you have a lucid dream you know you're in a dream even while you are dreaming. As your consciousness becomes aware you are dreaming you are more able to manipulate imaginary experiences, change outcomes in your reality and travel through the dimensions of the esoteric planes; you are dreaming your dreams awake! It can be great fun as you get to do all things you can't do with physical limitations, such as flying across the universe on your unicorn or swimming in the depths of the ocean.

More experienced lucid dreamers can control their dreams and often choose to visit particular places. I've walked into my sister's room deliberately during a dream and spoken to her while she was lucid dreaming too.

Those you love who have passed over can sometimes visit you in a dream. They often appear to be more alive than they were before they died, or have chosen to look younger. It's not always easy for them to appear to you as they have their own soul lessons to learn, so it can take them a bit of effort.

You should high vibe yourself just as you would for the unicorns if you wish to meet up with your departed loved ones in your dreams. They will come with messages and sometimes with apologies if they want to say sorry to you for something. It's always such a delight to meet up with them, and unless you are consciously lucid dreaming it's often sad to wake up to find it was all a dream. Fear not, for it would have been a real meeting between you both but just in a different dimension.

Dream journal

It's not always easy to remember details of dreams, which is why keeping a dream journal next to your bed is most important. Record your dreams on a regular basis and track the themes and patterns. You will find your dream journal is a unique personal treasure filled with an invaluable source of insight into your nightly activities, including recurring dreams and your travels with the unicorns.

Dreaming mind

When you go to bed always do so with a sense of excitement, for you will be going on a journey as you always do whether you are aware of it or not. The dreaming mind is an expansive creative force of the entire consciousness of the universe, so please don't dismiss the dreams you have for each one is entwined with meaning and messages to assist you in your awakened state.

It is important you acknowledge your dreams, for while you are in this state you are experiencing a divine association that enables you to truly connect with the soul being you really are. A newfound awareness and perception will open doors to many realms, and you will discover there is no beginning and no end, that everything is limitless.

Pay attention to your dreams, for your dreams are valid. Go to bed with a clear conscience. Trust the messages and visions you receive, and keep a dream journal next to your bed so you can make notes of your dream-time experiences.

Unicorns, Mother of Moon
I ask for my wishes to come about soon
I'll drink of the moon this very night
With loving heart and open sight
Change I embrace, show me your ways
As I become one with every moon phase.

Unicorn dreams

Unicorns always come from a higher perspective and will accompany you to the etheric planes, where you are able to have visions and memories of high experiences. Unicorns always look for those who shine purely and brightly, and will search for those they can

work with. Remember that unicorns cannot lower their vibration so they will look for those who have a glimmer of the qualities they have, such as compassion, dignity and honour, or for those who shine brightly.

One way to invite the unicorns in at night-time is to visualise a column of bright light going from your bed all the way up to the roof outside. It will light you up and make it easier for the unicorns to find you and come in. Imagine the column as being as bright as you wish, and keep it clear as you infuse it with your prayers, love and best intentions. It will act as a portal for the unicorns to reach you easily when you go to bed.

Unicorns love to meet us on the inner planes during our dreams. Dreams about them are usually extremely vivid and colourful and feel real, as though they are happening on the physical plane.

Many years ago after one of my workshops, one of the participants dreamt of a unicorn. She said the feeling she got from the unicorn was one of absolute purity. It gently nuzzled her, and she said that its smell was different to that of a horse. The only way she could describe its scent was to say that it was comforting, like no other. She explained to me that she never usually remembered dreams but this one had been so vivid, as though it was real. The strength of the dream has stayed with her and she can still smell the unicorn from time to time; it takes her straight back to her connection with the unicorn, which really did visited her in her dream.

It's incredible how you are able to go into different worlds and how those worlds can cross into yours when you are asleep. One night I dreamt that I was searching for my black cat, Anubis. He is so dear and gentle and an absolute darling. 'Anubis! Anubis! Anubis!' I said to him in my dream. I called out to Anubis to come to me.

As I continued to call my cat, the wall in my room split into two and a thick mist seeped through the gap. I felt a dark, dark energy and Anubis, the black jackal, the Egyptian god of the underworld, appeared. I was absolutely terrified! A strong magnetic force pulled me towards the wall, and I tried to hang on to the legs of my bed as much as I could. It was too strong for me so I called with all my might to the archangel Michael, my go-to angel of protection, for his immediate help.

Just as I was being pulled through the wall a unicorn dashed in and pulled me back from the wall just in the nick of time. He was cobalt blue, the same colour as Michael's aura, a colour of protection, strength and courage. I woke up scared, relieved and exhausted all at the same time. I was so thankful to have survived that ordeal.

It was more than a dream; I had connected with the afterlife, which is just next door in another dimension. I had escaped to within an inch of my life, for there is no return from a visit to the underworld. It was a unicorn that had saved me, that pulled me back from a power that was too strong for me. Since then I have never ever doubted the strength of a unicorn, and I have to say I have never been so pleased to see one either!

I have never used Anubis' name lightly since whenever I call for or speak with my cat. There is energy in every name, as we already discovered, and an immense power in the names of the deities, who are to be fully honoured and respected.

Just because we may experience unicorns in an alternative reality doesn't make it any less real. When you meet one in your dreams it is a true soul connection, and they will often bestow you with a gift that will assist you towards enlightenment. As they work with you on a soul connection, the unicorns know exactly what you need in that moment of time in order to move forward. As they assist you in aligning to higher realms, magickal changes take place as you awaken to the unicorn energy. Try this unicorn meditation:

Winter is a mystical artist that adorns nature with jewels of sparkling frost and paints the landscape with glistening ice. It is a time when one's breath becomes visible on a cold, brisk day and leafless trees stand strong even though stark and bare. This is a season where mystery hangs in the air as dark nights draw in, enveloping the weakened, low-slung sun. It is a time of looking deep within, a time of hope and a belief in magick.

In your mind's eye you find yourself in bed preparing for a night-time adventure. As you drift off to sleep you find yourself chanting:

This season's magick is laid bare
And in it I would like to share
Unicorns take me by the hand
Fly me to winter wonderland.

You notice that a large bedroom window has been opened wide into the dark night's sky. You shiver at the cold crisp air that near takes your breath away, and look out across at the full moon hanging in the deep velvety night. In the distance you see a bright light glinting and moving swiftly through the darkness. You feel compelled to follow it with your eyes, and whisper:

Keep the light and shine it bright
Keep the truth with all your might
Keep the light and shine it bright
Drawing healing from this night.

Suddenly, with a gust of wind and a sprinkling of magick, you find yourself flying high across the sky on the back of a unicorn. Oh, what great fun! It soars easily like a bird over black silhouetted rooftops towards a forest. This is a forest like no other for everything is frosted silver, with sparkling fir trees below you and the ground glistening in the light of the stars.

You land and find yourself in a clearing deep within the forest, and your eyes adjust as you look up. A soft glow of moonlight floods your face from above. Bathe in its soft, gentle energy as you become immersed in the divine feminine, which opens up your heart chakra like a beautiful rose. Feel any old habits, behaviours, fears and thought patterns that have been preventing you in moving forward fully now dissolve. This is the unicorn's opportunity to help make your dreams come true, as it gifts you with the presence of receptivity.

As the moon continues to stream its sacred light you start to feel a force field of silver spinning around you in a circle. Stand strong within this energy of unicorn and moon enchantment, and let the magickal workings unfold. Listen to what the unicorn has to say, as it may give you advice or instructions, and allow it to grant your wishes in its own unique way.

Some fairy folk approach with a beautiful goblet that bears the moon's image; they tell you this is in honour of the moon goddess. They offer you the goblet, which is filled with liquid moonlight. You take it, and as you sip its qualities of intuition, integrity, peace, love, compassion, femininity, receptivity, confidence and a higher ability pour into you. Hand the goblet back and take a moment as the energies you have just consumed are assimilated into your essence.

Drink of the moon on this fine night
With open heart and loving sight
Go forth and be the real you
Upon the dawn, may dreams come true.

As you make your wishes, the pure feminine energy of the moon is received into your body. Feel every cell awaken to and assimilate with the powerful receptive energy of unicorn moon magick as you become as one with them.

You look up in gratitude to the unicorn and become embraced by the comfort of its unconditional love. You truly shimmer as the unicorn moon magick sets to work, as your vibration lifts to the higher frequency of the unicorn realm.

Gently you are lifted up and realise that the unicorn is carrying you through a magickal rainbow that bridges the dimensions from your dream to the physical world. Breathe in the colours as they stream through you. Feel the energy of the magick of the wishes you have just made as the unicorn returns you through the open bedroom window.

Dawn has risen, and as you start to stir in your warm bed quietly reflect on all that was revealed to you in the night as you dream your dreams awake!

CHAPTER 4

UNICORN HEALING MAGICK

T K
THIELMAN KERVER

Crystals, chakras, magick spell
Assist the outcome very well
Glowing horns of shining light
Third eye opens, sacred sight
Restore, balance, soothe the soul
Affirming all is healed and whole.

The unicorns are coming to us now, during this time of great change in our world, to teach and show us the gift of unconditional love and the power of healing. They guide us in waves of ascension energy to connect us with their radiant light and heal us on an emotional level.

The healing power of unicorns enables you to let go of your ego self so you can step into your true authenticity. There's a unique and unmistakable power in knowing, becoming and being your real self. Transformational healing is the gift of the unicorns, which will invigorate you on a spiritual level and make you feel more connected with your higher self. Most of all, as you receive the pure energies of the unicorns' healing it will trigger your innocence, your original divine essence, so that you can attain the blueprint of soul, connecting you to who you truly are.

Unicorns offer their nurturing and loving care to enable you to stand in totality and balance, thus giving you the natural strength and ability to help all those in need without draining your very own life force energy. When you are healed and whole, the world that is directly around you also becomes healed and whole. When this is understood and practised, then it is healing mastery.

Unicorn healing message

Your soul's cry for healing help has been heard! For our sensitivity picks up on the discord of hurt, pain and suffering, as well as the torment of grief. However, fear not, for the effectiveness of our bright healing light has the power to knit together a fragmented heart, to bring about wholeness and emotional freedom. Our magickal bedside manner will ensure you are healed in time. So take comfort in knowing that the peace you crave will soon be restored. In the meanwhile, rest within our protection, as we nurture and care for you.

Heal well, dear one, and never, ever give up.

The compassionate healing love of unicorns helps soothe discomfort and encourages you to investigate the beneficial healing properties of natural remedies by seeking out a qualified herbalist, or indulge in natural energy healing practices such as the unicorn healing energy method.

One of the magickal gifts a unicorn can bestow upon you is the skill of a healer. Their healing light is a powerful strength that you can use to heal yourself, others and the world around you. But before you can heal anyone it is important to heal yourself first. The healing energy of the unicorns is a very high vibrational frequency. Once you are cleared of any emotional pain that is holding you back from your own ascension, you are more able to assist others. Working with the unicorn empowerment ceremony exercise outlined in Chapter 1 will help you to eliminate any negative emotions.

Nature

Unicorns have a special affinity with nature, and weave their healing magick through every season. They call to those who naturally hear their whispers though the breeze, who welcome the rains, glorify in the heat of the sun and connect with the nourishment of the earth. The unicorns invite you to venture through forests, meadows and parks until your heart sings once more at the mere notion of the magick of nature. Allow them to awaken your affinity with the ways of natural healing and to seal your belief in the natural workings of miracles and magick.

When you step outside you connect with a shining world within your own, of fairy elementals, rock spirits, crystal spirits, guardians of the lakes, streams and oceans and spirits of the forests, meadows and mountains. Our ancestors lived their lives trusting in the spirits of the land and lived in accordance to the magickal law of nature.

You can connect to the healing energy of the unicorns by tuning into and connecting with the outside world. When you work with unicorn healing in this way, you can incorporate the energy of the four basic elements and the spirits of nature. We all know that nature in itself is healing. Whenever you go outside and smell the fresh air, hug a tree or sniff a flower, you benefit from the healing properties that nature naturally emits. It is a unique restoration that allows you to unify body, mind and spirit with the elemental spirits of nature.

Healing this way allows a deep connection with Mother Earth and our natural state of being and wholeness. Here is a unicorn elemental releasing exercise:

- Light a black candle under a dark moon.
- Hold an amethyst crystal to provide you with soothing emotional and transformational support as you let go.

- Imagine you are standing within a circle of light for protection. Say:

With arms outstretched this very night
All hail dark moon, now void of light
Emotions placed in the crystal, clear
Intentions set, release all fear
Spirits of earth, I stand my ground
Spirits of air, sweep all around
Spirits of fire, shine brightly within
Spirits of water, gift me discipline
Unicorns now restore my glow
With thanks to nature, I let go.

- Place your fears, doubts and worries into the crystal itself. Leave it under a dark moon to face the elements as your emotional ailments are released and healed.
- Let the candle burn right down, and say:

Mother Nature, hear my call
For the higher good of all.

Chakras

Chakras are energy points found in your subtle body in which your life force energy flows through. Those who are attuned to energy healing systems such as reiki work to heal, cleanse and balance the chakras to bring about wholeness and balance.

The seven main chakras are aligned centrally though the body. Each chakra has its own colour (etheric) that represents its own metaphysical energy. If a chakra is out of alignment due to negativity, fearful thoughts, beliefs and doubts surrounding what the chakra represents it will cause imbalance, which can affect us on every level including manifesting physical dis-ease. For example, worrying about paying bills could cause your base chakra to become stagnant, as this is the energy point that represents security and material needs. Fearful thoughts and a belief in lack will cause this chakra to become unbalanced, which could manifest into physical pain or dis-ease such as lower back problems.

Because the chakras represent your spiritual life force, they can arguably play an even more influential role in dictating your emotions and mental health. They dictate whether you feel vibrant and full of life or lethargic and down in the dumps, depending on their condition. It is vital that any stagnant energy is released so that a flow of vital and fresh energy is restored into the body. Aligning your chakras so they're perfectly balanced and in tune with each other helps to get you feeling highly energised and connected to higher spiritual beings such as the unicorns.

The etheric of each chakra is as follows:

- *red*: base or root chakra; safety, survival, security, grounding, material needs
- *orange*: sacral chakra; emotions, creativity, sexuality, flow.
- *yellow*: solar plexus chakra; confidence, personal power, will
- *green*: heart chakra; love, empathy, compassion, relationships
- *blue*: throat chakra; truth, creative expression, communication
- *indigo*: third eye chakra; intuition, extrasensory perception, inner wisdom
- *purple*: crown chakra; universal connection, spirituality, consciousness.

When all of our chakras are healed we are in alignment with the whole of who we are.

This is a quick and easy way to balance and heal the subtle energies for body, mind and spirit:

- Create a safe and quiet sacred space.
- Light a white candle and play soft ambient music.

- Lie down and invite a unicorn in. It breathes a white light down through your crown chakra, illuminating each of your chakra points.
- Visualise each of your chakra points.
- Imagine each chakra spinning in a clockwise direction.
- Focus on each one in turn.
- See the individual colour of each becoming more vibrant.
- Visualise the colour extinguishing any darkness caused by negativity that might be blocking the flow of energy, preventing a chakra from spinning freely.
- As the unicorn focuses on cleansing and activating your chakras, become receptive to its healing light.
- Relax and rest as you become restored to a place of balance and wholeness.

If you feel your psychic abilities need to improve or that you're out of balance on any level, you can send beams of light to your chakras. For instance, if your personal power and self-confidence needs a boost, beam a yellow healing light towards your solar plexus chakra. Breathe the light in and see it cleansing and clearing away any blockages until it is illuminated fully. Work with all of the chakras in the same way as you beam the corresponding colours to each in turn.

Each of the intuitive senses corresponds to the body's chakra system. Once your chakras are healed your spiritual gifts and psychic abilities will improve, enabling you to receive the loving messages of the unicorns.

Clairsentience is intuition that comes through emotional or a physical sense of feeling; it corresponds with the heart chakra. When you are whole, healed and balanced, messages from the unicorns are received through feelings and emotions.

Claircognisance is intuition that comes from a strong ability of knowing; it corresponds with the crown chakra. When you are whole, healed and balanced unicorns will download divine information into your mind and you will just 'know' without having learned it in the conventional way.

Clairaudience is intuition that comes from a clear ability to hear divine guidance; it corresponds with the ear chakras, which are situated on your temples on either side of your face. When you are whole, healed and balanced you receive communication through the loving words of the unicorns and relevant messages through songs and phrases.

Clairvoyance is intuition that comes from a clear sense of seeing; it corresponds with the third eye chakra. When you are whole, healed and balanced unicorns will deliver their messages through visions in your mind's eye, dreams and via physical signs.

A unicorn is a gleaming being of purity, beauty and unconditional love whose strength lies in its horn, for this is where its healing power is stored. The magickal healing properties of the horn are purifying, cleansing, medicinal, curative and protective. They are said to eliminate poisons, and have the innate power to draw away dark black energy and turn it into the brightest, luminescent light. A unicorn's horn dissolves and heals the deepest soul wounds, and can clear karma from many lifetimes. This can be a very freeing and powerful healing experience. A unicorn's horn was named an alicorn in mediaeval times, although this was taken from the Italian word for unicorn, *alicorno*.

Located at the centre of the forehead, the unicorn's horn symbolises your third eye chakra. While your two physical eyes see the past and the present, the magickal third eye works with the pineal gland to reveal visions and insights to the future. It is your birthright to harness the visual gifts that have remained dormant within your mind's eye for far too long. When a unicorn touches your third eye chakra with its horn you may become aware of an interconnectedness with all things, truth in all situations will light up and you'll feel a deep, deep contentment.

The unicorns have returned now to assist you in awakening your very own alicorn, and to restore and magnify the power of your spiritual sight. Try this unicorn third eye awakening exercise:

Bring your focus to your heart centre and breathe love in and out as you make a connection with the unicorn realm. As you start to relax, allow your imagination to open up. Mists billow all around, and you marvel at how mystical the grove you find yourself in looks at this time of dusk.

Towards you through the twilight steps a glowing unicorn. You gasp at the sight and tremble in its purity as it approaches you. With a nod of its head you are led to a beautiful birch tree, and feel compelled to sit. Your back leans against the rough bark of the silver birch and you make yourself comfortable.

The unicorn comes to you and gently places its horn upon your third eye. Immediately, a bright white light blazes through your third eye, clearing away old debris and blockages that were caused by fear. The unicorn assures you that it is safe to use your sacred sight in this lifetime.

It breathes its breath upon you, which has the power to purify and transmute negative, lower energies and transform all your fears relating to your spiritual sight, in all directions of time, into high frequency light.

As the light expands your third eye becomes awash with divine healing energy and fills with colours of violet and indigo and flashes of silver sparkles, unveiling illusions and truth. And so your spiritual sight starts its journey, enabling you to truly see the past, your future and the truth in all situations. It is time to trust in the subtle messages of the unicorns as new spiritual doorways open to awaken your psychic abilities.

With your physical eyes closed, watch as vivid images screen through your forehead until you fall into a deep and restorative sleep.

Usually a unicorn's horn is seen as pure white, to match its glossy coat, mane and tail along with the powerfully pure attributes and qualities of the unicorn itself. As previously mentioned, there are unicorns of different colours that will appear to you if and when you require the properties of the energy of that colour, and that also goes for horn. However, unicorns grow and evolve spiritually through service, and a golden horn indicates the greatest wisdom attainable.

Unicorn Healing Energy System® attunement

A unicorn's horn possesses magickal powers consisting of pure divine energy that radiates and heals on a deep soul level. You can supercharge your healing sessions to an even greater level once you are attuned to the Unicorn Energy Healing System®, which will assist you with the age-old secret and unique healing energies of unicorns.

Usually the attunement is initiated personally by myself during my unicorn therapies and workshops; however, special unicorn permission has been granted for this sacred initiation to be shared within these pages to connect you to the powerful healing energy of unicorns to enhance your own healing flow. The sacred unicorn symbol should be used with reverence and sanctity.

- Sit quietly and take three deep cleansing breaths in and out.
- Imagine a beautiful stream of sparkling white light pouring down through your crown chakra through the top of your head.
- See your head become illumined from inside out with this light of the divine as its energy travels down through your body, cleansing, energising and balancing each chakra in turn.
- Using your power finger (the index finger of your writing hand), draw a circle on your forehead.
- As you continue to circle round clockwise with your finger pull your finger away, making smaller circles to form the point of an etheric spiral; this is your bright glowing unicorn horn.
- Draw the unicorn horn symbol into your palm chakras in the same way as described above.
- Place your hands together in a prayer position.

Namaste.

Once you have received the unicorn healing energy attunement you will be able to call upon unicorns at any time to assist you in transferring their magickal energies into yourself or your client.

Now that your healing abilities are enhanced with the pure energy of the unicorns, a powerful golden healing light will naturally stream through your enteric horn as well as your hands. At the start of any session, visualise the sacred horn symbol shining brightly and protruding from your forehead and from your palm chakras. The healing energies and guidance from the unicorns will pass through your hands to where healing is needed. As you pass their healing energies through your hands you may also notice messages of guidance that come through your intuitive senses from the unicorns, for yourself or to share with your client if you have a healing practice already.

Follow this method for a unicorn healing energy attunement:

- Play a relaxing ambient music CD.
- Light a rose incense stick and some white candles.
- Place unicorn crystals around the therapy couch or bed.
- Call in some powerful unicorn energy by saying:

Magickal beings of high energy
Lend me your powers, and assist me

Guide and show me where to place hands of light
Reveal any ailments and enhance my insight
Healing of unicorns goes deep to the soul
Health is restored, now fully whole.

- Imagine a strong golden light coming out of your hands; this is the pure unconditional healing light of the unicorns.
- Place your hands on each chakra in turn.
- In your mind, see the light pour through your hands into each energy point as you focus on restored health on every level for the person being healed.
- As you work this way with the unicorns please don't ignore anything that comes up for you on an emotional level, as it could be a sign for yourself or for the person you are working on. When you have finished, imagine a large glowing white unicorn horn being placed around the client or yourself to keep the beautiful healing qualities intact and safeguarded.
- Drink a glass of water or offer it to your client and say:

I give thanks to the unicorns of purity
and accept this healing most graciously.

You are able to activate the healing power any time you visualise or focus on the symbols in your hands and forehead. The attunement can never be revoked, so the energies are with you for life and beyond!

Crystals

Now that you are flowing and glowing, why not use unicorn crystals for healing?

- *Clear quartz*: place a clear quartz crystal on your third eye chakra. Cover it over with your palms in a hand healing position. Focus on visualising the sacred horn symbol to activate the flow and glow of unicorn healing to remove blockages and to open sacred sight.
- *Rose quartz*: place a rose quartz crystal on your heart chakra. Cover it over with the palms of your hands. As you focus on the symbol, connect with the healing love energy of the unicorns.
- *Selenite*: place a selenite crystal upon your solar plexus chakra and cover it with your hands. Focus on the symbol as the healing flows through the crystal, cleansing negativity and instilling peace and alignment with the unicorns.

- *Jelly opal*: place a jelly opal crystal upon your throat chakra, and cover it over with healing hands. Focus on the symbol to heal any blockages to community with the unicorns and to raise your vibration.
- *Snowy quartz*: hold a snowy quartz crystal in activated hands during mediation to facilitate clarity and receptivity.

As you continue to work with the healing light of the unicorns you will feel a deep sense of peace and contentment, which is infinitely beautiful for body, mind and soul.

Unicorn essence

Sometimes the natural unicorn in us can't cope with the lower frequency of non-magickal muggles. Although you have the ability to lower your energy (unlike the unicorns) to fit in with others, it will only make you low and miserable and it's obviously better if your vibes are shining and high. When you are brought down by those around you refusing to open their hearts to the purity of the unicorns, or when you want to feel that 'unicorn thing' going, just spray some unicorn essence into your aura.

Unicorn essence is filled with holy water infused with unicorn blessings, crystal elixir and essential oils that resonate with the unicorns' characteristics and frequency. Spraying it into your aura or space enables unicorns to come nearer to you and touch you, which means you can absorb their energy at a cellular level. You can also offer it to others for healing.

Unicorn essences are simple to make but are a super-high frequency solution when you need a quick unicorn fix! You will need:

- unicorn crystals of your choice plus ionised water (you can buy this at a chemist, or simply use cold water that has previously been boiled)
- holy water (if you have it)
- pure alcohol (cheap vodka works well)
- 30 ml green-coloured bottle with a spray top
- essential oils such as bergamot, frankincense and ylang ylang (this is my favourite blend for super connection with the unicorns, but feel free to experiment and choose your own)
- tiny unicorn crystals (optional)

Pop the unicorn crystals into the ionised water to soak overnight (apart from selenite, which will dissolve in water). Bless and pray over the water, then add a couple of drops of the water if you have it. Fill the spray bottle three-quarters of the way up with ionised water. Add in a couple of drops of pure alcohol.

Add 20 drops of bergamot, 15 drops of frankincense and 12 drops of ylang ylang. Sprinkle the tiny crystals into the water if you are using them. Twist the lid on tightly and shake the bottle.

Your unicorn essence is ready to spray into your aura or healing space, to use for room clearing and bringing in a vibration that matches the qualities of the unicorns.

Psychic protection

Whenever you work with magick it is vitally important that you protect yourself. Having awakened to the magick of the unicorns, you are most probably super sensitive.

For psychic protection benefits imagine yourself being encased in a beautiful, hard, enlarged unicorn horn. See it as bright and luminous, almost blinding, and choose the colour you feel you need (drawing from the unicorn colour list in Chapter 2).

Visualise the horn surrounding your body and aura to serve as protection against any harsh and lower energies that come your way. You can also retreat within the horn when the going gets really tough. Add some bling to your horn by imagining glittering and sparkling with a light of purple or white around it, for added protection.

Grounding

Before partaking in any spiritual work, whether it's meditation, invocation or any other form, you must ground yourself. Unicorns love our planet and would like to see you attached to it rather than floating off into the ether. Going outside into nature and standing barefooted on the ground will instantly ground and connect you to the element of earth.

Imagine strong roots growing from the soles of your feet. Watch in your mind's eye as they bury deep into the ground, growing stronger and longer until they reach the centre of the earth. Visualise a huge crystal there, take note of what it looks like and let your roots wrap around it.

Breathe up the crystalline energy and the earth magick and allow it to surge through every part of your being. You are now grounded and ready to connect with unicorn healing magick.

Unicorn waterfall of healing magick

Unicorns often work in groups and will appear in a circle when concentrating their healing energy towards a person. Their powerful horns light up as they help heal your emotions, balance your chakras and heal you on an intense soul level. Unicorn colours are vivid and intense, matching the restorative qualities of these magickal healers.

Unicorns beam their powerful healing energy out to the world to restore balance; they work with us in the same way. If your delicate system is clogged with the harshness of negativity or unhealthy consumption, the unicorns offer to supercharge your chakras to bring about optimum health and psychic awareness.

It is time to take a visit to the unicorn waterfall of healing to receive an energetic overhaul as the unicorns supercharge you with the healing light of their horns. Take a few deep breaths in and out, close your eyes and relax . . .

You find yourself in a beautiful forest, and as you walk into a clearing you notice a pretty waterfall that cascades into a beautiful pool of the clearest water. Bathing within the pure waters are seven white unicorns, each with a different-coloured horn. You gasp at the sight and sit on the soft grass to watch them. As you bask in the warmth of the sun, you lie back and relax in the magickal energy of the grove.

Out from the pool steps a gentle white unicorn whose horn glows with the deepest colour of red. It gently bends its head and touches your base chakra with its alicorn. The red light beams through your base chakra, healing the energy point from any of the issues you have relating to safety,

security and material needs. Breathe in the red light and allow the healing to take place as your base chakra becomes whole and healed. Restore!

A unicorn whose horn glows the brightest orange softly touches your sacral chakra. Immediately you see the area fill with a luminescent orange colour as it heals your thoughts and feelings about addictions and appearance and creativity issues, and how you think of yourself. Breathe in the orange light and allow the healing to take place as your sacral chakra becomes whole and healed. Let go!

A unicorn with a horn that glows like the sun touches your solar plexus chakra with a light of golden yellow. The colour rushes through the energy point, healing any of your issues to do with personal power, will and self-control. Breathe in the yellow light and allow the healing to take place as your solar plexus chakra becomes whole and healed. Relax!

Stepping from the pool next is a unicorn whose horn is deep emerald green. As it touches your heart chakra a healing green light beams through your heart centre, healing any of your love, relationship, emotional and people attachment concerns. Breathe in the emerald green light and allow the healing to take place as your heart chakra becomes whole and healed. Breathe!

A beautiful light blue-horned unicorn flicks its tail and beams its light towards your throat chakra. As your neck lights up the colour rushes through, healing any of your issues relating to speaking your truth, communication and creative expression. Breathe in the blue light and allow the healing to take place as your heart chakra becomes whole and healed. Be calm!

A unicorn whose horn flows the colour of indigo steps towards you and sends a light of the same colour toward your third eye chakra, in between your two physical eyes. Your forehead fills with a deep indigo blue, lighting up your third eye as it heals any issues you may have concerning your future, the past, your desire to see through the veil and opening your spiritual sight. Breathe in the indigo light and allow the healing to take place as your third eye chakra becomes whole and healed. See the beauty!

A unicorn whose horn lights up with the colour of royal purple bends its head towards yours. It places its purple horn on the top of your head and beams its light down through your crown chakra. Feel this area fill with vivid royal purple as the colour rushes through you, expanding, cleansing and healing this energy point that represents the creator, spirituality, divine guidance, knowledge and trust. Breathe in the purple light

and allow the healing to take place as your crown chakra becomes whole and healed. Be the power!

All seven unicorns stand around you now in a circle with their heads down and their colourful horns pointing towards a corresponding chakra. Feel the power as the unicorns light you up.

A powerful vortex of energy emerges from your third eye, and a spiral cone shape of golden light extends forth. As though you were plugged directly into their consciousness, you clearly hear and feel messages the unicorns have for you and watch the colourful visions stream through your mind's eye.

Each chakra is perfectly cleansed and you feel this perfect rainbow of unicorn healing streaming through you from the base of your spine to the crown of your head. Breathe in the colours, and feel the energy and the magick of the wishes you have just made. As you rise to your feet and stand firmly on the ground, the rainbow expands outwards and you feel the energy of the mighty unicorns before you. You watch as a rainbow of colours swirls around the unicorns, reflecting upon the crystal clear surface of the pool.

As the unicorns move closer together you sit up, and they lift their heads so that the tip of each horn touches above your head. Waves of pure unicorn energy blaze all the way down through your body and back up and out of your crown chakra, purifying your energy and all aspects of your higher self.

Shine brightly as they infuse your energy with this healing and powerful magick that is divine love. Focus on your breathing and enjoy the restoration as you merge with the pure shimmering light.

When you feel that the process is complete, give thanks to the unicorns.

Open your eyes when you are ready, knowing that you have just received a most rejuvenating treatment at the unicorn waterfall of healing.

CHAPTER 5

UNICORN SERVICE MAGIC

Healing stars fill up the sky
Heightened senses, vibes are high
Personal power is the key
Authenticity sets you free
Restore and mend with hands of light
Service helps the world stay bright.

As the powerful unicorn healing energy continues to blaze through you, and the more you work and connect with unicorns, you may find that your sensitivity heightens even more than it is already. The energetic vibration of unicorns is a very high frequency, and as you harness the unicorn qualities the higher your frequency will rise to nearer match that of the unicorns. It will make communication easier, and your magickal healing work more effective and powerful.

A unicorn's sensory faculty is so high it is literally off the scale, for their senses can pick up on anything way beyond your capacity. It's no surprise they have a highly evolved sense of hearing, and can pick up sounds that people are unable to hear.

Unicorn senses

Unicorn means 'one horn', from *uni*, meaning 'one', and *cornus*, meaning 'horn'. In a similar way, *universe* means 'one verse' or 'one song'.

Every living thing in the universe has its own individual note or tone, and each note or tone resonates with the energy of each specific being. The grass emits its own sound as it grows, as does the sun when it rises, the planets when they move and the stars as they twinkle in the sky. They all send out music, as does the whole of creation; this is the sound of the universe. In the beginning was the *sound*, and it became manifest as the original primordial sound diversified and became many.

Each separate vibration evolved to reflect the whole of the all, in infinite disguises, giving rise to the world in which we live. Universes within universes, each vibrating at their own frequency, interact with every other frequency to produce the variety of life.

Unicorns can hear the music of the spheres, the melody of running water, the whispered songs of the four winds and the heavenly choir of angels singing. Unicorns can hear it all.

Unicorns love to be in nature, not only for its harmonising energy but because of the beautiful healing notes and tones that it emits. Every part of nature has its own unique sound, as it blooms and withers and changes with the seasons. Unicorns love to listen to the full orchestra of the rhythms of nature.

Colours too have their own sound. For instance, yellow may sound mellow or perhaps as a high vibrational squeak. Use your senses to determine how you feel colours may sound. Imagine the translucent way a peach-coloured rose looks, and the changes in colour that take effect when the sun shines through its petals in a way that makes it glow. How would that sound to a unicorn?

Gardens for unicorns

If you wish to invite the unicorns into your backyard, make sure your garden is unicorn friendly. A garden full of colourful flowers, a lush lawn and trickling water feature emanates the most sublime musical notes, which is healing for the planet and attractive to unicorns. Make your garden a riot of colour for you and the unicorns to enjoy. As you plant flowers with colours bursting into bloom or fading after pollination, the orchestra of nature continues to play.

Flowers bring to unicorns the sacred gift of colour and fragrance, and are a natural source of cosmic energy that you can draw upon whether you are aware of it or not. Unicorns urge us to literally 'smell the roses'! The natural healing power of the rose will penetrate deep into your heart, opening up your awareness to divine love.

Every flower variety has its own restorative properties and unique healing ability as well as its own sound, which unicorns can hear throughout their life cycle. Planting unicorn flowers such as roses, lavender and lilies in your garden will encourage unicorns to come in their droves, and will add an extra sparkle of magick into your backyard.

It is time to bring the beauty of unicorn flowers into your life. Try this **unicorn flower invocation**:

- Hold the head of a flower of your choice in cupped hands. As you gaze into it say:

  I call upon this unicorn flower
  Bestow upon me your magickal powers
  I breathe in the fragrance, filling my heart
  Beauty surrounds me, ne'er to depart
  Enhance my senses so I can hear
  Your floral tune play in my ear.

- Now breathe in the fragrance deeply and say:

I work your magick, with harm to none
To heal and restore me; there, it is done.

As you know yourself it can be extremely difficult when you are highly sensitive. Can you imagine how hard it is for a unicorn, whose senses are uber sensitised? Whereas anything that is high vibrational is sweet sounding and euphonious to a unicorn, the tones of a lower frequency can be repelling. An untidy and lifeless garden full of rubbish would sound discordant to unicorns, as they are far too sensitive to cope with an absolute din.

Sounds and smells

Every organ, tissue, and cell has a vibration that, when in harmony, creates the most wonderful symphony imaginable in your human body. Your aura also plays musical notes, the quality of which depends on the state of it.

Whenever disharmony arises or an interruption of the vibration occurs there's a loss of wholeness leading to discomfort and dis-ease, but with the right sounds you can align yourself with the vibrations that foster health, happiness and unity. This is why it is so important to keep your vibrations high. Whenever you feel down and negative your very own unique note will sound discordant to the unicorns and they will stay away.

Our emotions have a sound, and also a smell! Anger sounds like an aggressive bark to the unicorns, and smells acidic; jealousy growls and smells of ammonia. This is not at all pleasant for unicorns, and they avoid you at all costs when you indulge in lower-energy emotions – they detest discord and stench. Remember next time you get angry or seethe with envy to have consideration for the poor unicorns. Can you imagine the sound and smell you're giving off? On the other hand, unicorns absolutely bliss out on the sound of purring and the perfumed fragrance that the qualities of love, happiness and joy radiate.

Shine the light! Unicorns hear and respond to the energy and the intention of all sounds and smells, so be sure to always keep that in mind. Make sure they are attracted to you and not repelled. Try your best to keep shining, and don't allow your light to dim.

High vibration is linked to the positivity, love, compassion and peacefulness of unicorns; your vibration impacts on your relationship with them. Remember that the higher your vibration the more authentic you become, and the unicorns will be drawn to anyone who is genuine. Don't be afraid to be yourself, for you are at your most powerful when you become your authentic self.

Authenticity is about staying true to what you believe, and being brave enough to express your genuine feelings and opinions. Unicorns want you to drop the act, to stop trying to people please so that you can shine as the individual star you truly are.

Every time a lie is told the truth is concealed, or when you gossip about your friends your vibration lowers and the unicorns will go out of their way to avoid you. As already outlined, they cannot lower their energy to accommodate you when your energy is linked to fear, anxiety, sadness, depression or any other negativity. However, they will turn up in droves and add their magick wherever there is uplifting music, harmonious singing, sacred ritual, chanting, lit incense, flowers, essential oils and anything else that raises positive energy. Continual connection with the unicorns will keep your frequency high, as will honing your unicorn qualities. Don't forget too that a quick spray of homemade unicorn essence will open your up to their light.

Unicorns always come from a higher perspective. They are attracted to pure light and will search the planet for someone who shines a pure radiance of unicorn qualities to work with. They will look for those who wish to offer their service, who dedicate their time and prayers to helping others and to those who desire to make a difference in the world.

If you'd like unicorns to come to you when you are in bed visualise a beautiful stream of light coming from the night sky through the roof of your house and down into your bedroom. Fill the light with love, prayers and high intentions and it will act as a high vibrational portal that the unicorns will be easily able to access. It's a wonderful way to let them in, and they will see the shining column from their dimension.

It is impossible for unicorns to enter anywhere with a low negative energy; for example, prisons and hospitals are filled with the energy of fear. Fear is a root energy from which other lower emotions can develop, such as jealousy, anger, resentment or aggression. Schools, factories and other workplaces can be filled with a dreaded fear, particularly on a Monday – energies tend to be higher when it comes to Friday, when everyone clocks off for the weekend!

Even though unicorns can't lower their vibrations to enter such places, they still desire to spread their powerful healing magick. If there is just one person who has a pure heart, unicorn qualities or high vibrations through prayers and beliefs, the unicorns will see their light as an invitation to come in.

You can assist the unicorns too by creating portals of light in your imagination. By doing so, unicorns are able to travel down the column into the building in order to restore healing on all levels.

Causal chakra

When a unicorn sees your light of service shining above your crown chakra, it will connect automatically with you. If your causal chakra is open it will enter your energy fields through it, enabling you to channel its loving messages and guidance.

The causal chakra is a shimmering white moon and is known as the eighth chakra. Located just behind the rear of the skull, it is transcendent and sits between the crown and soul star chakra (the ninth chakra). This energy point was once physical along with the other seven chakras in Atlantean times. It is one of three transcendent chakra points, and as your light levels rise towards that of mastery the causal unites you with the fifth dimension. As the light within your soul grows brighter, the unicorns bring in even higher aspects of themselves through your causal chakra.

Like the unicorns, the causal chakra is a magnet for lunar light while also absorbing and radiating divine feminine light. As unicorns return, they usher in the vibration of the deep feminine compassion and wisdom of Atlantis. They work with the moon to pour the powerful silver light into the hearts and minds of humanity, to assist in awakening your causal chakra in preparation for a pending new golden age.

The unicorns help to activate and anchor the causal chakra in order to bring you great peace, comfort and inspiration from the higher realms. If you are experiencing a great shift in your personal energy, you may find that what you once found attractive no longer appeals to you as your sensitivity increases. Everything you are feeling is entirely natural,

for it is your wish and desire to spiritually evolve that has brought about these changes in you. As you connect with the unicorns practise meditation, say daily prayers and live your truth; your vibrational frequency will rise to match the psychic phenomena you seek. It is time to trust in the subtle messages of the unicorns as they guide you towards a new spiritual awakening.

For this **unicorn causal chakra awakening** exercise you may wish to work with the crystal kyanite, which acts as a bridge to the unicorn realm. Holding a piece above your head will create a channel for higher frequencies and upgrade your psychic senses and spiritual gifts. It is a perfect tool to assist in awakening the causal chakra, and will help to increase your intuition and connection with the unicorn realm.

Hold a piece of kyanite with arms outstretched to a full moon at midnight and say:

Mystical moon of feminine light
Gift me your wisdom, upon this fine night
Moonbeams invited to stream through my crown
Fill me with magick, all the way down
Awakening chakras, opening wide
Sacred connection stirs deeply inside.
Causal ignites to now activate
Unicorn magick determines my fate

Spiritual connection upon midnight hour
I now fully claim my unicorn power!

Service

'The best way to find yourself is to lose yourself in the service of others.'

– Mahatma Gandhi

When you truly give from the heart, you are working from the perception of the bigger picture. When you give of yourself in service your soul becomes nourished, allowing you to expand beyond earthly limitations. True joy lies in the act of giving, and it is a wonderful way to bond with the unicorn realm. Giving is a great investment towards achieving genuine peace and happiness, and you'll find that in return the unicorns will ensure you are provided for on all levels.

If it feels as though you are being called to offer your services to assist the unicorns in planetary healing, then be sure to spread light, peace, harmony and joy wherever you go.

After having the unicorn attunement (see Chapter 4) your hands will be filled with the divine light energy of the unicorns, and you can effortlessly channel their healing magick. Feel your hands shimmer and sparkle and sense them tingling. The magickal energies of unicorns easily flow out from your etheric horn in your third eye chakra. Ethereally,

this is seen as a radiant golden light with shimmering stars that sprinkle over anywhere the light is directed. See the pure luminous energy build in your mind's eye, or feel it and then send it out across the world to all in need of the healing magick of unicorns.

Light a candle and ask the unicorns to help you absorb the rays of light as pure unicorn energy floods through into your aura.

Accept any healing offered to you, for unicorn energy has the power to release and transmute anything that is out of alignment with your life purpose. As you anchor the light it will stay in your aura, raising your vibes and igniting your chakra system.

It is time to light up the world in love, peace and balance.

Unicorn planetary healing meditation

Sitting comfortably, close your eyes and relax as you take a few deep breaths in and out. As you continue to breathe deeply, a thin circle of golden light forms around you. Say:

Unicorns, unicorns! May we unite
Against all fears, let us shine our light
And wrap it with love around the world
So healing's revealed and peace is unfurled.

You become awash with the purest peace you have ever felt and your heart begins to glow as you breathe in and out deeply. The heart light expands, and as it does you become completely filled with this pure and peaceful healing energy. As the light continues to expand from you further it pushes up into the skies, and a pure white unicorn travels down through the portal to meet you.

You immediately feel its qualities of beauty, compassion and love as it invites you to climb up onto its back. Feel the unicorn energies flow through your entire body as your merge with it as one. The unicorn takes off into the air, and twinkling golden stars flow out of its horn as your hands and forehead tingle in the magickal energy.

As the unicorn glides high across the skies you focus on the mountains, towns, deserts, forests, rivers and creeks below and send an abundance of magickal healing stars from your hands to cover these places. As they begin to fill, you nod your head to direct beams of healing light from your ethereal horn with your highest intention, so that love and healing blessings are received.

The healing light energy continues to pulse through you and spreads rapidly to every part of Mother Earth as you continue to direct it across the

lands. The light expands out across the oceans, cleansing and purifying the waters.

Further up and out into the atmosphere the golden light continues to spread. It wraps around the planet's aura like a blanket of healing, and lifts the planet's frequency to that of a higher consciousness to awaken the hearts and minds of humankind and reveal a healed wholeness of peace and love.

You feel exhilarated from your journey as your unicorn places you down and enfolds you in a beautiful soft pink light. Bathe in this healing light of calibration as it integrates you with the higher healing and love energies of the unicorns.

As a thank you for your continued service, the unicorn gently nuzzles you and you say your goodbyes, for now. You profusely thank the unicorn and it disappears back up through the column of light.
Take a deep breath and gently open your eyes as you receive the unicorns' heartfelt gratitude for the very real and much needed healing work you have just offered to the entire world. ♥
Namaste.

CHAPTER 6

SPREADING THE MAGICK

Shine out brightly like the sun
Exude confidence and fun
Ride through rainbows; seek, explore
Limitations are no more
Authenticity is key
Time to claim your destiny.

Tonight, look out into the night sky and observe the constellations shining back at you. You can create your own destiny if you wish to, but it is the stars that point you in the right direction of your dreams. With this in mind, take some time to decide what it is you wish to come true.

Unicorns grant wishes to those who ask, so that peace is created and happiness attained. A wish is a magickal gift, a plea and request that is delivered to the one who has desired and asked for it. However, some wishes are made that will never come true because the wishmaker did not fully believe their wish would come to fruition.

How many wishes have you made in your lifetime, and how many of those wishes have actually come true?

Believe! Believe! Believe!

So often you wish upon a star, but then negate your request for fearing it might not happen. Immediately the doubt blocks your wish from coming true. This fear stems from a refusal to believe that anything is conceivable, but when you work with unicorns remember that everything is possible – even the impossible!

What would you like to ask for? What help from unicorns do you need to become the best version of yourself? Try this **unicorn wish incantation**:

Unicorns will take me far
I'll make a wish upon a star
Wisdom's found now deep inside
Higher self's my perfect guide
Believe and trust, it will come true
Dreams and goals are realised too
With eyes closed I'll count to three
Magick's made, now wait and see.

Think of ways to be the best you can be. Remember to stay true to who you are and never allow others to take away your power. When your words are dissed or when your actions are mocked, your light fades because you don't stand up to be counted. The unicorns urge you to step into your authenticity so you can grow and evolve fully. When you step wholly into your personal power, destiny presents itself. Take this opportunity to focus on a lifelong dream or ambition knowing that you will be supported fully by the unicorns as they breathe clarity through your heart and mind to reveal your next steps.

You have an important life purpose and are here to shine brightly. Trusting in your intuition as you work with unicorns will help you to embrace life and live it to the full. The light of your inner knowing beckons you as you take bold and positive steps towards your dreams and goals. A glittering new gateway has opened, and you are invited to step through it into a shining new world that has been waiting for you.

As the unicorns come out to greet you they highlight the rainbow path you are to take. Enjoy every precious moment, knowing and appreciating that you are totally blessed and will continue to be so as you continue to assist the world of the unicorns while adding your own illumination and magickal touch.

Unicorn blessings

Unicorns symbolise success and open you up to infinite possibilities and freedom. As they gift you the wisdom to see through their eyes, you are more able to step into your authenticity and away from the limitations of fear. Whenever you call upon the magickal power of unicorns they give you their blessings to ensure the best possible outcome for the higher good.

Whenever you wish for anyone to experience the pure energies of unicorns, you are actually offering them a blessing. The unicorns will guide you to direct the shining unicorn healing magick from your hands or spiralling horn towards anywhere that needs it. As you go about your day shine brightly, and offer the purity of the unicorns to all that you see. Send the healing magick from your hands, and watch in your mind's eye it surround and fill all those you direct it towards. As you drive, one nod of the head will send out divine light from your etheric horn to anyone or anything you intend it for. You can also do your healing work during meditation, as we did in Chapter 5, and fly over the world, showering it with the unicorn healing energy from your hands or spiralled horn as you fly overhead.

Remember to work with the unicorns by imagining portals of light over anywhere that might hold dark energy, such as prisons, hospitals, factories, office and government buildings, housing estates and social establishments. This will assist the higher energies of the unicorns to flow in and help balance the energies of aggression and negativity. If there is just one person pure enough in these places, a unicorn can enter the portal and work with that person to ignite the light the person holds, to bring hope and enough illumination to touch others.

When you call upon the unicorns to bless a person or situation, you can be sure that a unicorn will send showers of love and hope. Remember that everything you send out comes back to you one hundredfold, so open yourself up to receive great blessings from the unicorns as you give with a joyful heart.

Keep your vibrations high, so that your light is seen from the unicorn realm. Create an altar dedicated to the unicorn realm. Place upon it white flowers such as lilies and roses, unicorn figurines, unicorn crystals, incense and candles. This is your sacred space for honouring, connection and focus. Whenever you walk past it you will be reminded of the unicorns and light up.

Say your prayers for the world, light candles, chant sacred mantras, burn incense, talk about unicorns, think about unicorns, read about unicorns and spread the healing magick of the unicorns to truly light up your life, as well as the whole world.

Unicorn prayer

Dear unicorns

Please continue to bless and protect me as I focus on the divine light within myself and all others that I meet.

Help me to see through your eyes as I awaken to your loving messages and guidance. I graciously receive your healing magick with an open heart in gratitude.

Help me to serve, help me to shine.

In love and honour

It is so. And so it is!

Awaken, dear ones, from your slumber and allow us to ignite the divine flame of light in your heart. Shine brightly as we assist you in illuminating the way.

– The unicorns

IMAGE CREDITS

Chapter openers: Domenichino, 1602, *A virgin with a unicorn*, Wikipedia, https://en.wikipedia.org/wiki/File:DomenichinounicornPalFarnese.jpg

Page vi: Bewick, T. 1790, *Unicorn wearing a crown*, wood engraving, British Museum, https://www.britishmuseum.org/research/collection_online/collection_object_details/collection_image_gallery.aspx?assetId=1612943674&objectId=3549095&partId=1

Page 2: Raw Pixel, *Vintage unicorn illustration*, Flickr, https://www.flickr.com/photos/vintage_illustration/46785851121

Page 34: Lambspring, 1625, *Red deer and unicorn in a forest*, Wikimeda, https://commons.wikimedia.org/wiki/File:Licorne_et_cerf.jpg

Page 62: Wellcome Images, 1551, *A unicorn woodcut after C. Gessner*, http://catalogue.wellcomelibrary.org/record=b1198805

Page 83: Morphart Creation, *Girl writing*, Shutterstock, https://www.shutterstock.com/image-vector/girl-writing-pen-rested-against-her-1384759202

Page 94: Kerver, T. circa 1500, *A brief history of wood-engraving from its invention*, Wikimedia, https://commons.wikimedia.org/wiki/File:Brief_History_of_Wood-engraving_Thielman_Kerver_Mark.png

Page 122: Schonguer, M. circa 1400, *Seated lady holding a shield with a unicorn*, Picryl, https://picryl.com/media/seated-lady-holding-a-shield-with-an-unicorn-5ba575

Page 140: Master of the Amsterdam Cabinet, circa 1473, *A wild woman on a unicorn*, Rijksmuseum, https://www.rijksmuseum.nl/en/collection/RP-P-OB-915

Other products by Flavia ...

ISBN 978-1-925682-43-4

Discover how to tap into the magickal energy frequency of the mermaids to enhance every aspect of your life.

ABOUT THE AUTHOR

FLAVIA KATE PETERS is known as The Fairy Seer who embraces the mystical path of the Old Ways. A teacher of natural and ancient magick, Flavia is the founder of the Unicorn Energy Healing System® and trains others through her magickal professional certification courses at the College of Psychic Studies, London, and across the globe. She is a regular presenter on the mind-body-spirit and pagan circuits and regularly graces the pages of *Spirit and Destiny* magazine, *FAE Magazine* and *Witchcraft & Wicca*. Television appearances include *Celebrity Haunted Hotel* and *Lightworker's Guide to the Galaxy*, along with various guest slots for BBC Radio. Flavia's authentic and honest approach makes her a most sought-after wisdom keeper, and her mission is to keep the magick alive! She shares a mystical shop with fellow author Barbara Meiklejohn-Free and their magickal cats Anubis and Sekhmet, in Buxton, UK.

www.flaviakatepeters.com